Praise for *ROE Powers ROI*

ROE Powers ROI provides the key to ensuring business success in today's world.

—Vince Poscente
New York Times best-selling author, *The Age of Speed*

ROE Powers ROI is a new and important contribution to business and management literature. It lays out a novel and compelling vision for how a CEO can get the best and most collaborative outcomes from the management team.

—Charles D. Connor
President and CEO, American Lung Association

ROE Powers ROI will change the way you think and enhance your communication skills whether in the boardroom, in the store, at home, or at a party. Presented in easy-to-understand terms, the ROE methodology can be implemented by anyone, anytime, anywhere. The bottom line is this book will increase your effectiveness, pure and simple.

—Tom Ziglar
CEO and proud son of Zig Ziglar

Innovative, invigorating, and right-on, Michael Rose's *ROE Powers ROI* will enhance the way you think forever. This book should come with a highlighter. Read, reread, and progress.

—Dean Lindsay
Author, *The Progress Challenge and Cracking the Networking CODE*

The ROE methodology helped my team better understand our business and leadership principles. It is a powerful tool that has encouraged participation and adoption of our key business objectives that will support the success of Wingstop Restaurants.

—Lance Loshelder
CFO, Wingstop Restaurants

Presented in easy-to-understand terms, the ROE methodology can be implemented by anyone who desires to enhance their way of thinking and communicating with others, regardless of the situation.

—Paul Spiegelman
Founder and CEO, The Beryl Companies

Michael Rose has really attacked and solved a serious problem for most business—achieving a greater return on energy. Too many companies waste their resources and misuse their talent, which can put them out of business. Michael has developed a methodology to fix that once and for all. If you are running a business or are in a business, you really need to know and understand what Michael is teaching.

—Kent Billingsley
President, The Revenue Growth Company, Inc.

Leaders who value people development first and business results second will benefit from reading *ROE Powers ROI*. ROE impacts everyone within an organization and identifies the pain at all levels to break down the silos and get people talking. If you have a job but are looking for a promotion or another job altogether, ROE is for you.

—Tony Hartl
Founder, Planet Tan
Author, *Selling Sunshine: 75 Tips, Tools, and Tactics for Becoming a Wildly Successful Entrepreneur*

It is imperative that all companies both large and small maximize available resources, especially from their people. *ROE Powers ROI* provides the tools to make this happen. Having seen Mike's philosophy at work in my organizations, it is clear that managing energy is the key to productivity.

—Mitchell Allen
Serial entrepreneur and author

Return on Energy will do for management what Porter's Five Forces did for business strategy.

—Terri F. Maxwell
President and CEO, Succeed on Purpose

I enjoyed the exposure to Rose's ideas as I have also engaged these challenges both as a CEO and as a consultant and advisor. I can see how ROE would give a management team a new way of thinking about their business, the organization of their people and processes, and their communication with each other.

—Don Arnwine
Retired CEO, VHA

Having been present at the birth of Michael Rose's three "Ways," it's particularly exciting and gratifying to watch how he developed these key concepts into a business leadership toolkit for any company leader who is looking to implement growth strategies.

—Andy Birol
Birol Growth Consulting
Author, *The Five Catalysts of Seven Figure Growth*

ROE

POWERS ROI

The ultimate  WAY
to think and communicate
for ridiculous results.

R. Michael Rose

Brown Books Publishing Group
Dallas, Texas

ROE Powers ROI™
The Ultimate Way to Think and Communicate for Ridiculous Results

Brown Books Publishing Group
16250 Knoll Trail Drive, Suite 205
Dallas, Texas 75248
www.BrownBooks.com
(972) 381-0009

A New Era in Publishing™

ISBN 978-1-61254-021-4
Library of Congress Control Number 2011944296

Printing in the United States
10 9 8 7 6 5 4 3 2 1

To my parents, who gave me the gift of how to understand myself and relate to people, and especially to my wife, Nikole, who showed me how to embrace it to fulfill my life's purpose.

Contents

Foreword

Michael and I are pretty different. He lived most of his life in the populous states of Pennsylvania and Texas. I was born and raised on a small Caribbean island with less than 150,000 inhabitants. Michael studied at a small regional school in Texas and, after a short employment stint, became a successful entrepreneur. I took the road of Ivy League universities and top-five MBA programs—interspersed with employment at prominent investment banking and consulting groups. My most recent summer vacation took me to a place where I could practice four different languages; Michael took his family to the quiet serenity of the Colorado Mountains.

At first glance, you wouldn't think of our partnership as a match made in heaven, but the truth is that our relationship is highly effective, efficient, and enjoyable. We hit the ground running from day one and never looked back, and we have a great time working together. Some would call this a coincidence, or good fortune, and leave it at that. That's not good enough for me. I insist on understanding the root cause of everything, and then try to figure out if and how it can be replicated.

My first inclination was to validate whether our success was a matter of complementary skill sets and personalities along with a common objective—similar to what drove Disney's success in the late eighties and nineties when Michael Eisner (the strategic and creative visionary) joined forces with Frank Wells (the operational and financial expert). I quickly realized this is not the case for us, as Michael and I constantly trade hats and take on different roles when working together.

As I reflected on the ROE methodology Michael had previously shared with me, it became clear that we were living, breathing examples of the thinking and communication program he had developed. We intrinsically understand the three Ways of thinking and communicating he has identified, and shift seamlessly between Ways according to the need. For example, when trying to formulate a strategy, I need Michael to be the Way One and help him develop the vision. This helps me to be a qualified Way Two and develop the plans that will ultimately make the vision become a reality. For his part, Mike will routinely change from a Way One to a Way Three and help execute the plans that I have put together in my Way Two role. The real key to making these shifts successful is in changing not just the manner in which you think, but also your communications with the other person. The dialogue and questions between a Way One and a Way Two are radically different from those between two Way Ones, or between a Way Two and a Way Three. This is the magic of ROE, and why it is at the core of our successful working relationship: it provides practical tools to quickly diagnose and subsequently apply the right thinking and communication for *any* situation. Forget about expensive and extensive training programs; ROE delivers ridiculous results in a matter of hours by placing people in the right roles, clarifying the expectations for their role, and teaching them how to think and communicate accordingly.

So what can you expect after reading this book? Your first reaction will likely be to determine which Way best describes you and what that means for your current job situation. You will find yourself asking and answering whether you are in a position that capitalizes on your strengths, and whether those around you are in the right positions as well. You will likely then apply the tools from this book to evaluate the types and quality of communications that take place within your organization. Armed with this insight, you will formulate a clear point of view on your own and your company's growth trajectory; is everything looking good or is it time for a change?

Moving on, you will probably look at every person, organization, or company differently than you do today. As you meet and talk to people, you will find yourself silently classifying them as a Way One, Two, or Three; understanding their wants, needs, and concerns; and tailoring your own communications approach to most effectively engage with them and making sure you "speak their language." You will do the same as you look at organizational structures and management layers in clubs, churches, organizations, and companies—trying to understand why they are structured a certain way and quickly diagnosing problems that will now appear obvious and elementary.

These are just a few examples of how I believe this book may change those who read and adopt ROE. Having experienced these changes myself, and hearing the feedback from hundreds of ROE seminar participants, I am excited to see the impact this book will have on the broader audience. I congratulate you on taking this important step for your personal and professional development and trust you will enjoy this book.

—Menno Ellis

Acknowledgments

I want to thank God for giving me the gift of insight to develop the material in this book from three simple words in 2007: return on energy. My purpose in life is to help those who want to help themselves. This book marks the start of fulfilling this purpose.

My wife, Nikole Rose, and I are partners in life and business. Rose Group Companies is running strong under her leadership. Without her amazing skills for running the company, I would not have been able to focus my attention on the book you hold in your hands. For that, I am eternally grateful. But her involvement goes way beyond managing a business. Every entrepreneur needs unwavering support at home. She made me think many years ago that I could do this—even before I thought I could. Thank you for your unconditional love and support. Honey, I love you so much. Your name should be on the cover.

My parents, Jack and Janett Rose, both passed away within three months of each other last year. My dad missed the publication of this book by fifteen months. I owe so much gratitude to them. I grew up in a small business. They gave me my e-gene (entrepreneurial genetics). They also gave me the gift that provided me with the necessary awareness to develop the content for this book. They worked so hard in their business for very little return. Mom and Dad, your return came a generation late. I will always work to make you proud and pay it forward.

My kids and stepkids, Lauren, Sydney, Ryan, and Preston. You guys give me so much hope for the future. Thanks for your understanding and support in having an entrepreneurial father, as well as your understanding of all the additional time it took to write this book. Thank you also for enduring all of our vision, strategy, and tactics talk.

To my amazing in-laws (yes, I said amazing in-laws), Kathy and Devon Medlang. Thank you for raising such an amazing woman. Your own accomplishments and life disciplines have inspired me in so many ways.

Because I have a degree in biochemistry, I sometimes refer to Rose Group Companies as my ROE laboratory. The ROE methodology has been developed using real-life experiences in managing and growing a business. Thank you to all past and current employees for teaching me so much about business. This book is a result of the knowledge I received from you.

I also have to thank all the Rose Group Companies clients. I have learned so much from all of your business challenges over the past fourteen years. ROE was initially developed to deliver value to you in a very commoditized business. I am very proud to have Rose Group Companies powered by ROE to serve your needs.

This book would not have been possible without the Entrepreneur Organization, and specifically my EO forum, BottomLine: Randy Haran, Rob Jones, Jeff Frankel, Clint Herzog, Mike Kahley, Chris Brown, and Greg Coon. I have learned so much from your life experiences. Your unconditional love and nonjudgmental support will never go underappreciated.

Thank you to Milli Brown and everyone at Brown Books Publishing Group. You have been a great partner and educator throughout this process. I can't wait to do it again!

Introduction

ROE

Times are tough, but that's not news. Neither is the fact that the economy is precarious, sales are declining, profits are stunted, people are frustrated, and it's just a great big mess out there. Being a business owner, consultant, and advisor, I've had the advantage of observing both successful and failed businesses and comparing results from the experience. What I learned is this: the number one problem isn't poor marketing strategies, outlandish ideas, or a lack of consumers. In *Good to Great,* Jim Collins says that a major problem with struggling companies is that they put the wrong people in the wrong seats on the bus. ROE takes it a step further by defining what those seats are and the right way to think and communicate in those seats.

In other words, the wrong thinkers are filling the wrong positions. As a result, miscommunication and confusion abound during a time when the economy is at its most unforgiving.

Along with this realization came a solution involving three simple words: Return on Energy™. ROE is a methodology developed to get the right people into the right seats and maximize your organization's success, or return on investment. What few people realize is that there are three distinct roles that compose any successful organization, and those roles are determined by "Ways" of thinking and communicating: Way One, the visionary; Way Two, the strategist; and Way Three, the tactician.

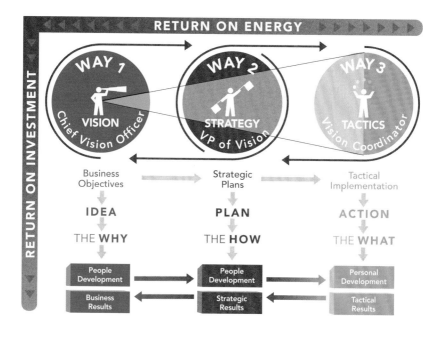

At the core of Return on Energy—or more to the point, a major compound of its core DNA—is return on investment. As you will no doubt gather by reading this book, we believe that positive return on investment is locked up inside true ROE. In other words, those who follow and practice ROE will inevitably achieve a higher return on investment in their company—and in their life as well.

The beauty of ROE is its sheer simplicity once you recognize and implement the Ways. And yet there are thousands of people and businesses that continue to struggle day-to-day to survive when all they need is this clear understanding of who is best suited for each Way in their company.

Take the logo at the opening of this introduction, for instance. I have shown this logo to hundreds of people in the course of preparing this book, and very few actually see the ROE without prompting. Instead, they only notice the ROI—return on investment. Just like these struggling businesses, they see only the desired profit and overlook the key to achieving this goal. Their surprise when I point out the ROE to them is actually pretty entertaining, but more importantly, it provides me with a teachable moment where I can successfully convey one of the central tenants of ROE: when you look at business, you generally see ROI first, too.

When you set up your processes and training to increase Return on Energy, you will find that ROI naturally increases as well—once you understand the Ways and that ROE means recognizing and implementing them and a new way of thinking about business, the people in it, and their desired results. ROE is a translational tool, a decoder of sorts. You can use it to translate everything in the business world. It's the tool for increasing ROE because you're going to the core of the challenge or the problem and using a universal language unencumbered by cultural baggage, business jargon, or the smokescreens employed by those who seek to obfuscate rather than illuminate.

SECTION I

Can't You See the Arrow?

one

Awareness

*It's not the events that matter most to us, but rather,
it's how we interpret those events that will determine how we think
about ourselves and how we will act in the future.*
—Anthony Robbins

From an early age there was something different about how I saw the people around me, how I learned to communicate with them, and how I watched them communicate with each other. My childhood couldn't be a more typical American story. I grew up in a small town in Pennsylvania, I worked in my father's deli, and I was fortunate enough to be the first person in my family to go to college. So my ability to recognize and resolve business ailments isn't necessarily anything that's been passed down to me, nor is it some innate superpower.

If anything, it probably started with what my dad taught me when I worked the counter at his deli. Picture a nine-year-old being told by his father that when you're talking to a customer, you look them in the eye and remember that everyone in the world is wearing an invisible sign that says, "I want to feel special."

Looking back, I think that's a better inheritance than if he had handed me a check for $1 million.

For the longest time, right up through college, I didn't really look very far out into the future. I picked a college to apply to based on something a friend said in the car on the way to a concert in our senior year of high school. I picked a major—biochemistry—that was far removed from business, because I'd seen how hard my dad worked at running a business and I thought it was the last thing I wanted to do. But even in a world of serious-minded, tunnel-vision academics and hyper-focused scientists in ophthalmology, I always found myself focusing on the people around me. I discovered it wasn't usual for people to move so easily among fellow students, fellow athletes, professors, and managers—all with very different mind-sets and different ways of thinking.

I realized that I had this way of observing people where I could tell what wave they communicated on. This continued when I started law school studies at night while working in a biochemistry lab in ophthalmological research and development during the day. I'd go to dinner and I might not notice whether my meal was prepared well, but I would know before the check came which couples were having conflicts, which couples were on their first dates, whether the server was having a good night, and if the bartender was having personal problems.

My way of observing people was sort of like when you see a picture of what looks like two candlesticks, only then you refocus your eyes and realize you're looking at two profiles in silhouette. Or like seeing the arrow in the FedEx logo, the *31* in the Baskin Robbins logo, or the arrow pointing from *A* to *Z* in the Amazon. com logo. Once you see it, you can't *not* see it.

Around this time, the entrepreneurial drive that was so much of my father's being finally kicked in with me. My e-gene activated and I started to see what I'd been blind to in myself, in the same way that I was sometimes blind to something right in front of me while at the same time I was able to see into people.

Idea. Action. Plan.

IDEA ➡ PLAN ➡ ACTION

I never paid much attention to at least a two of those, not to mention the order, and when it all clicked for me I saw the relationship in the achievement of an objective—whether it's at the personal level, being an entrepreneur, or working with a large organization. I started seeing how those who supply vision had to communicate with those who could form a strategy to accomplish that vision, and how those strategizers needed to communicate to those who had to carry out the specific tasks within the strategic plan.

Why should you care about this? How does my own unique perspective affect or impact you?

Simple enough. What I created over the course of the next four years is a methodology and an approach that is adaptable, objective, and measurable. Once codified, understood, and integrated, it's a filter that lets you see what's really going on with communications in a business venture. It's like in the original *Matrix* movie, when the character Neo finally saw through the computer code that constituted the virtual reality in which he lived. Once he saw through it, he was no longer subject to its limits and he could manipulate it to his benefit. Again, once he saw it, he couldn't *not* see it.

When I'm in a client's office or at a social gathering and I find myself with the frontline employees, I can immediately connect with them because I talk to them about what they do—how they impact strategy—and ask them how they could do their job better.

When I find myself with people in roles such as director or vice president, I talk to them about their strategic plan, how well that plan is being implemented, and the business objectives they are aligned to for the year.

When I'm at a table of CEOs and presidents, I talk to them about where they want to take their companies over the course of the next five years, or how they see their businesses evolving based on long-term trends and large-scale technological innovations measured in decades.

3

I can do this because everyone has a way of seeing things and a way of thinking about what they do.

I can't stress this enough. When I speak of a Way—and I capitalize it because it's at the core of this book—it is not a judgment, nor is it a measure of a person's value, nor is it a static state that people cannot grow beyond. It is not hierarchical, nor is it a virtual caste system. A Way is not necessarily endemic to the function a person performs, but it arises from their role. No one is stuck in one Way or another. In fact, some of the problems businesses face arise from the fact that people are communicating to each other in the wrong Way.

Way Ones are the people who provide the vision and set the business objectives. In a sense, the Way One has the easiest job of all. I like to remind people that ideas are easy; planning and implementation is what keeps you up at night. Of course, it's not really that easy—everyone has big ideas, but few have the vision for workable ideas and the force of passion to bring it to realization.

Way Twos are the people who create and plan the strategy that aligns with the vision and the business objectives to bring the idea to action. A plan bridges idea to action.

> Sometimes we miss the most obvious things in our quest for unnecessary complexity.

Way Threes are the action officers, the people who perform the tasks that accomplish the steps that make up the strategy.

If this seems like it's oversimplified or self-evident, stay with me. That arrow in the FedEx logo or the arrow pointing from *A* to *Z* in the Amazon.com logo should have been self-evident, but most people don't see it until it's pointed out. Sometimes we miss the most obvious things in our quest for unnecessary complexity. Sometimes the self-evident gets buried under so much meaningless jargon and so many business buzzwords that we don't see how we're talking right past each other and not connecting at all. How many times have you heard someone throw out a term like "brainstorming, " "think outside the box," "bounce an idea," or "in over your head," and you just nodded along, even though those phrases really don't hold the same meaning when you break them down?

This is the Way to get past all that. This is the Way to see things differently, to think differently, to process information differently, and to communicate differently. This is the Way to think in the twenty-first century. If this sounds too intangible, it isn't. Once you can see the Way, you can see right through all of the confusion and noise.

It appears that each person has a different translation for these familiar but confusing terms. Understanding the three Ways allows you to employ the methodology of Return on Energy—ROE. The methodology is your translational tool to fully grasp and incorporate ROE. ROE is the Intel™ inside. ROE is how people within an organization communicate with one another and how most writers try to communicate with you. But most of the time, these people speak different languages.

ROE is just as important as ROI. There's a causal relationship, really—a positive feedback loop that increases one with the increase of the other. In fact, ROE powers ROI.

This puts the Ways and means in perspective and allows you to see where you fit. I have gone through the ROE methodology over a thousand times over four years and have hundreds of case studies that have proven the effectiveness of the methodology. Maybe it's the scientist in me that wants to keep experimenting, changing one variable at a time until it works perfectly.

ROE and seeing the Ways are not ephemeral, subjective states or some business fad dressed up in new terms. These are objective tools. ROE is very real and it's directly tied to your bottom line, your ROI. If, as the saying goes, time is money, then ROE is time.

Here are some questions to consider as you progress throughout the book:

- How far out have you looked in your life, business, or job?
- Do you have a plan to get to where you want to be?
- What steps do you take on a daily basis?
- Do you observe the people around you in a nonjudgmental way?
- What are you blind to in yourself?
- Where are your FedEx arrows?
- Do you have more ideas, plans, or action items?
- How are you communicating with people at work?
- How do they communicate with you?
- What is the answer when you ask yourself, "Can I do better at my job?"
- Is planning part of your day?
- Is your focus less than a year, one year, or more than a year?
- Are you constantly coming up with big ideas?
- Where do you fit in the office?

It isn't my job to answer these questions, but to help *you* answer them as we proceed. As you learn about the three Ways and how they function in relationship to one another, you'll discover the true Way to smoother performance, higher profits, and better results. As your ROE increases, you'll watch an exponential increase in your ROI, too.

Are you prepared to break through the jargon and the buzzwords and implement a methodology that really works? Are you ready to take your business and your career to a whole new level of success?

If the answer is yes, then let's begin.

SECTION II

A New Way of Thinking

two

ROE: Return on Energy

Individual commitment to a group
effort—that is what makes a team work, a company
work, a society work, a civilization work
—Vince Lombardi

Imagine sailing a ship back in the era of exploration. It's one thing to say, "I want to sail beyond that horizon," but to actually make the trip, it takes bravery and the conviction that whatever is beyond the horizon is a prize worth seeking. However, to make it a successful trip, one must have a plan of action. This begins with devising a strategy. What sort of ship could make it that far? What kind of crew is needed? What kind of supplies will we need to get there? Will there be a banquet there welcoming us, or should we pack extra sandwiches?

A captain cannot meet all of these demands on his own. He needs a navigator to tell him which way to turn the steering wheel in order to stay on course. He needs a first mate to gather and command a crew that will in turn run the ship. Together as a whole, all positions work to reach that vision beyond the horizon.

But what if you have a disgruntled crew? What if your navigator doesn't have a clear understanding of your vision? Not only will you go off course, you run the risk of mutiny as well.

Return on Energy is a way of ensuring that your ship stays on course so that everyone may benefit from the riches of discovery.

ROE is represented by three basic tenets: vision, strategies, and tactics—or you could say ideas, plans, and actions.

In our world today, we are inundated with terms that don't really make sense. You start to wonder if they're just throwing words together to sound more officious or even to veil their own confusion.

For example, one that I hear a lot: "Strategic tasks."

What?

Well, which is it? Strategy or a task?

Is this plotting a course with a sextant or something to do with cleaning a sail at this moment? Is this plotting a way to increase sales by 20 percent by the end of the quarter or doing a follow-up customer service call?

It's one or the other. Too many people get inundated with these words and concepts and the responsibilities they imply when really it can all be broken down into three simple seats: Way One, Way Two, and Way Three. Understanding the different roles and characteristics of each seat leads to greater ROE.

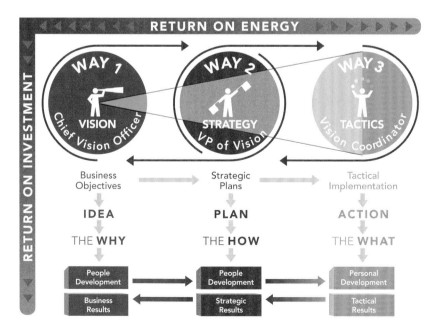

Return on Energy is a translational tool to decipher all the potentially great and not-so-great information at our fingertips today. ROE puts ideas into action by enabling the right thinking and communication with the right person. It allows not only for clear communication within the flow of command, but overall success and an increased ROI like never before. ROE is not a fad marketing tool, but one that will change your business with amazing results.

three

Way One: Chief Vision Officer

Good business leaders create a vision, articulate the vision, passionately own the vision, and relentlessly drive it to completion.
—Jack Welch

A leader has the vision and conviction that a dream can be achieved. He inspires the power and energy to get it done.
—Ralph Nader

The Way Ones are the chief vision officers. They are the dreamers, the innovators, and the grand architects. They are the idea men and women who see a problem or a challenge and say, "Why not?" They are the entrepreneurs who are able to come along and do what others have adamantly said could not be done.

The Way One contributes the vision, which describes a milestone that the firm will reach sometime in the future. Vision is a forward-oriented, long-term view, and its scope is as broad as the horizon. In fact, this vision may require decades to fulfill, but Way Ones are the reason businesses are able to make plans as far out as ninety-year leases and twenty-year objectives.

Not everyone can see the same vision as the Way One. Instead, it is the responsibility of the Way One to see everything from, as the saying goes, "forty thousand feet." Their job isn't so much to focus on the details, but rather on the end goal. However, this goal has to be a living, growing vision; otherwise, it is unlikely that the organization will continue to be successful.

Henry Ford was a Way One thinker. If he had asked people at the time what they wanted, they would have said, "Faster horses." Ford, on the other hand, envisioned a world in which the automobile was within the reach of everyday people. And he achieved just that. He had the pioneering spirit to persevere against the odds and establish an entirely new industry that has become a tenet of modern living. What Ford lacked, however, was the ability to evolve that is crucial to every Way One in order to survive the natural ebb and flow of business. As a result, Ford, the founder of the automobile industry, was overtaken by General Motors in the 1930s.

Texas Instruments was the standard of calculating machines in the 1950s and the 1960s, but failing to change with the technology revolution made them lose their place as a leading business tool provider. Only by remaking themselves in areas such as DLP technologies have they regained preeminence in the tech segment.

When Ford said he wanted to "democratize the automobile," that was the vision. But there were no specific quantitative goals or sales targets. When an entrepreneur says she wants to be the "Nike of the organic sports drink market," you can't exactly measure where the finish line is.

Therefore, the Way One not only creates the vision, but also a mission that incorporates the whole purpose for their enterprise or organization.

This includes the core values that are central to the firm. Core values reflect the deeply held principles of the organization that are independent of the current industry environment and management fads. A way to determine which values are core is to imagine the firm moving into a totally different industry. The ideals that remain intact in this new industry are the core values of the firm.

At the heart of these values is the core purpose, which is the very reason that the firm exists. This core purpose is expressed in a carefully formulated mission statement and is similarly independent of time and changes in the market. It is essentially the Way One's vision expressed on paper. It is what sets the firm apart from other firms in its industry and determines the direction in which the firm will proceed.

To sit in the Way One seat, you have to know a little of everything: how to manage financial statements, how to take ideas to action, how to set objectives, how to add new ideas when current ideas won't suffice—in other words, thinking "inside the box."

The most successful Way Ones, however, understand that people development is of the utmost importance in achieving business results. They realize that their ROE is contingent upon the ROE of their people. They ask more questions like, "Do you have the tools you need to do your job?" "What can I do to help make you more efficient, productive, happy, and so on?" and less questions like, "Where are sales today and what is our increase in gross profit margins?" They lead the people who write and manage the strategy, who in turn manage the people performing tasks. They are the idea architects—harbingers of all that can and may be.

> They lead the people who write and manage the strategy, who in turn manage the people performing tasks.

four

Way Two: Vice Presidents of Vision

People only see what they are prepared to see.
—Ralph Waldo Emerson

There are days when the Way Two will tell you it's like the lyrics to the Stealers Wheel hit from the 1970s: "Clowns to the left of me, jokers to the right, here I am stuck in the middle with you."

Conventional wisdom says that an idea without action is a pipe dream. But if the people who are performing the action do not have a list of well-thought-out steps or a documented plan for action, it could be very costly and an idea killer to boot. Moreover, it would lead to a poor ROE.

Way Twos are crucial on the path from idea to action. A Way Two thinks in terms of *how*. She creates the strategy to align with the business objectives.

> A strategy is the framework to enact and execute the vision.

A strategy, narrowly defined, means "the art of the general" (from the Greek *stratigos*). The Way Two is the general officer creating the invasion plans to accomplish the supreme commander's vision of breaching Fortress Europa. I like to call the Way Two "the VP of Vision."

Not only must Way Twos develop the strategy—they are also responsible for explaining the business to others in order to inform, motivate, and involve. They are responsible for benchmarking and performance monitoring. A strategy should not be confused with a vision. A strategy is the framework to enact and execute the vision. It is the how answer to the vision's *why*.

WHY ➡ HOW ➡ WHAT

A strategy is not the same thing as an operational plan or a task. A strategy should be broad, goal-oriented, and aimed in the direction and purpose of all the tasks that must be carried out to meet the strategy's objective. Compare the process of planning a vacation with what has to be done to go on vacation, such as packing, buying the tickets, and driving to the airport. Or think of a master chef, who will select the food concepts that support the owner's vision for the restaurant, work out the budget, and set the standards. The cooks are the ones who put the steak on the grill.

A satisfactory strategy or strategic plan, unlike the broad and long-term vision, must be specific, measurable, attainable, results-oriented, time-bound, and connected to the business results, such as an objective to increase sales by 10 percent by December, or to capture 5 percent market share of this new industry by the end of the fiscal year. They can relate to factors like market size, market share, products, finances, profitability, utilization, and efficiency.

The strategy that the Way Two provides is comprised of the rules and guidelines by which the vision is achieved, the mission completed, and the ideas executed. They can cover the business as a whole, including such matters as diversification, organic growth, or acquisition plans, or they can relate to primary matters in key functional areas. Way Twos turn ideas into SMART (specific, measurable, attainable, results, and time-bound) plans. You don't come to the table with one idea and leave with five ideas and no plans. That happens when everyone is thinking like a Way One.

Specific   Measurable   Attainable   Results   Timebound

19

Way Ones must be accountable to their Way Twos, and Way Twos have to be able to reign in their Way Ones. Way Ones are often sitting on ideas. They don't always think in terms of time limit, and they assume the Way Two is strategizing. A Way One has to deliver an idea with expectations. Otherwise it's like playing a game of business buzzword bingo, and the Way Twos leave the meeting having no idea what their next step is.

I know a vice president of marketing who develops comprehensive plans to fulfill a complex strategy aligned with the company's vision and objectives. Fine, right? Only her Way One CEO—a passionate leader—is someone constantly excited by new ideas. The CEO is often in the VP's office several times a week saying things like, "Oh, this company is trying this, let's include that in our campaign," or, "How can we add a social marketing aspect to this campaign?" The plans are constantly interrupted by changes. Eventually this VP had to bring her Way One under control, explaining why constantly tinkering would produce a Frankenstein campaign (unwieldy and ugly, not attractive) and that

> In order to increase their ROE, Way Twos must focus on strategy and explaining that strategy to others in order to inform, motivate, and involve.

while every idea she'd brought in was great, they couldn't be tacked on willy-nilly.

Some people in a Way Two seat have an even more challenging job. Whether it is because a business is so large that its regions or divisions are greatly autonomous, or because an organization is so small that one person has to wear several hats (there's another business buzz phraseology, meaning they have to think like several Ways each day), they sit in two seats at once. It's one thing to multitask, but you can't think in two Ways at the same time. It would be like running in two directions at once—you just end up running in circles. This is where many businesses make their mistake. In order to increase their ROE, Way Twos must focus on strategy and explaining that strategy to others in order to inform, motivate, and involve.

To sum it up, Way Twos are the ones who take that rough sketch and come up with a SMART strategic plan to accomplish the business objectives. Their skills include the following:

- Strong communication skills, both verbal and written
- Fairness with people and issues
- Consistency
- Objective, fact-based, unbiased decision making
- Ability to put those they manage first because they know employees are an asset, not a cost
- Detail-oriented mind-set
- Flexibility and open-mindedness
- Self-confidence to respectfully, properly challenge Way Ones and other Way Twos
- Understanding of their role as a Way Two
- Enough security and maturity to know the Way One needs a Way Two, not a competing Way One
- A strong enough ego to keep charge and allow their Way Threes to get credit for positive outcomes
- Process–oriented work ethic
- Ability to embrace change
- Feeling empowered by and accepting of responsibility
- Knowledge of how to write and manage plans, not just talk about them

If Way Ones are the architects, Way Twos are the chief foremen at the construction site. They devise the plan, gather the materials needed, organize the builders, and then put that plan into action. Their consistency, strength, and knowledge are what ultimately get the structure off the ground, manifesting the Way One's vision into reality.

five

Way Three: Vision Coordinators

Scientists dream about doing great things. Engineers do them.
—James A. Michener

The Way Threes are the vision coordinators. They are the *what* to the Way Twos' how. In many senses, they play the most important role in any organization. If you take care of the little things, the big things will take care of themselves, meaning if you pay attention to detail in carrying out tasks, then the business objectives will take care of themselves.

Way Threes have to perform these tasks as the action officers of their organization. Their role is where plan meets reality. And as any military person will tell you, no plan completely survives contact with reality. Regardless of the objectives, landscape, or your own organization's performance, something always fails to go exactly according to plan. Way Threes have to be able to perform their tasks, work cooperatively, and maintain a flexibility to ensure a task is completed despite unforeseen challenges. Adapt and overcome, as the marines say.

I'm an optimist by nature, and I have to believe that almost everyone in an organization comes to work wanting to do something well and to contribute to something larger than themselves. They want to feel that what they've dedicated their day, their career, or their life to has meaning. Those who don't—those who simply want to draw a paycheck or be free riders—are the exception.

Ideally, Way Threes have the virtues, characteristics, and skills necessary to realize their potential. They prioritize well, are good at time management, and are subject matter experts (SMEs) with their tools. They are good at resource allocation and they have an understanding of how the standards, expectations, and tasks before them contribute to the strategy and the vision of the organization. You'll notice that many of the characteristics on that list aren't general virtues, but they are specific to an organization. That's why it is so critical for organizations to commit to—and invest in—Way Threes.

Take Starbucks. They don't "sell coffee." The gas station "sells coffee," along with other items. Starbucks sells a place to come hang out. They sell a sense of community. The organization makes sure that their baristas understand this concept, and that is why the company puts so much emphasis on customer service training—at least as much effort as they put into training them on how to make lattes. A barista is a SME with the espresso machine. Baristas are taught how it all fits into the Starbucks mission, and it's why they are taught to be so genuine, conversational, upbeat, and welcoming.

Consider NASA engineers. A visionary, like Richard Branson, came up with the idea to create recreational trips to outer space, and his team of directors at Virgin came up with a business model, but it was the team of engineers who understood this vision and the directors' plans that made it possible for rocket ships to launch into outer space. They are excellent examples of Way Threes.

Way Threes who aren't highly motivated may not be that way by choice. Some have simply never been taught the basic skill sets needed to step into the responsibility of working toward a larger goal within an organization. This is why it is so important to have a qualified Way Two mentoring and managing a Way Three. Depending on the nature of the organization and its mission, this can be easily corrected if the Way Three is managed by a qualified Way Two thinker where people development is part of the vision of the organization.

BIG PICTURE

BIGGER PICTURE

25

Sometimes as a result of bad management, the Way Twos overseeing Way Threes never gave them an idea of how their role fit into the big picture and the strategy, giving them no sense of accomplishment in a job well done. Perhaps they followed every rule and directive, but because of turmoil at the Way Two or Way One juncture, the job became conflicting or directionless. For many reasons both voluntary or involuntary, many a strong and gifted Way Three has been turned into an unmotivated Way Three not performing to his or her full potential.

Want to see a great fictional illustration of how this happens? Consult pretty much any *Dilbert* cartoon. Way Threes, on the right side of the table, face many of the toughest challenges and are as critical to success as the Way One. They are the most important people to any organization. Remember, if you take care of the little things (the details), then the big ones (the strategy or business objectives) take care of themselves. An investment of time in those who occupy the Way Three seats, those with the characteristic to drink once led to water, is as critical as the investment of capital in any other aspect of the business.

> Those who sit in the Way Three seats are the people fueling the entire business.

The job of those who sit in a Way Three seat is not simply to perform some mindless task. If there's not a machine or app for such a task, there will be before you get done reading this book. No, those who sit in the Way Three seats are the people fueling the entire business, and what you need from the people who occupy those seats is far more crucial than the old idea of clock-punching worker bees.

A person in a Way Three seat is all about action. Planning and ideas aren't really what they need or have time to focus on. However, every Way should have ideas for their respective Way of thinking, which will lead to increased efficiency and better ROE.

Qualified Way Threes know why they are doing what they do. They communicate efficiently with the Way Two. They ask good questions. They have a vision of their role and therefore have ideas about how to improve their role and increase their ROE. If they are increasing their ROE then they are increasing the Way Two's ROE—what great motivation to mentor, because, yes, the ROE wave keeps going, ultimately increasing the Way One's ROE. So in effect, the Way Three can keep the boss's boss off their boss's back.

A qualified Way Three is very organized. They have great time management skills, and they can prioritize many different tasks. They have cultivated good listening and note-taking skills and can process information very quickly, even verbally. If I were to certify them in that type of role, I would take them through the kind of personal development training that may not directly have anything to do with the organization's products or services.

Way Threes are dependable, reliable, and trustworthy—virtues you would like all Ways to have. I think sometimes we delay making position changes due to the fact that the virtues of an individual are solid. But characteristics and skills are critical. Either someone has the skill or they don't. And the way to acquire the necessary skills is either to invest in yourself or to have a manager who recognizes good characteristics and prescribes the proper people development—i.e., mentor and manage. But in the case of the Way Three, they must want to learn and improve—a very important characteristic.

Everyone wants to be productive and feel like they're doing something important. But if their management, training, or communication is bad, a Way Three can easily become frustrated and disillusioned.

My first supervisor out of college considered sharing information a weakness—he was not big on people development, specifically on the mentoring side. I was a super-motivated Way Three. I entered my first job out of college as a research scientist and was going to come up with miraculous drugs that would cure eye diseases. My first day was an exciting one. I was at a big-name pharmaceutical company with unlimited resources. I was told I was one out of 250 applicants chosen for my position. I believed I possessed all the virtues and characteristics required to do great things and move up with the company to get more and more responsibility. To my alarm, my manager put me on washing laboratory glassware duty for two weeks. What his reasoning was I still don't know. And it never improved from there.

Despite that, my characteristics kicked in and I took it upon myself to meet many people and self-learn the skills necessary to accomplish my goals and the goals of my department. I was the first to the lab every morning. I read in the research and development library at lunchtime and on breaks. I went back and consulted with my college biochemistry professor, who was a great career mentor. My virtues would not allow me to permanently reside in the role of an unmotivated, nonplussed Way Three like many of the people I met.

After almost four years, in 1997, I decided to resign and start my company. It was only during my two weeks' notice term that people told me what a great job I had been doing. Some said, "Congratulations, you are getting out and pursuing a dream of entrepreneurship." One was a vice president who wanted me to reconsider, go get my PhD in polymer chemistry, and "move up the ranks." I left with one of the highest salary adjustments allowable. But all I wanted was to be developed, managed, and mentored by a qualified Way Two who understood the why of our department and would teach me how our department fit into the larger objectives of research (at the time about nine hundred scientists) and ancillary departments like development, quality assurance, clinical testing, and sales and marketing.

I could have, however, asked during the interview process how much people development experience my future manager had by asking strategic questions and noting how he tied them to my future tasks. I would like to have known from our departmental Way One where the company was going over the next twenty years. After all, I was willing to commit that long; I wanted to know if I should align my vision with the vision of the company. It is a great company. I admire their company's products and financial performance. Like many companies, however, an investment in people development—using the ROE methodology—will make them greater by focusing on ROE first.

In fact, during my new employee orientation with the company, the executive vice president of research and development stated in a short introductory video, "You could be sitting in my seat one day." I took that statement seriously. Motiva-

> Motivation should always be backed up by substance.

tion should always be backed up by substance. Very shortly thereafter I found myself as the Way One of my own company—talk about a change in a Way of thinking.

To return to our building analogy, Way Threes are the builders. They do the daily work of the company. Without them, there is no hope of breathing life into the Way One's vision and no tangible way to achieve the company's objectives. If ROE leads to growth—which it does—then Way Threes will always be better prepared to deal with the challenges and pressures of achieving both their goals and the organization's if they are trained, nurtured, and developed.

SECTION III

What Do These Words Mean Anyway?

six

Broken Arrows

To effectively communicate, we must realize that we are all different in the way we perceive the world and use this understanding as a guide to our communication with others.
—Anthony Robbins

Have you ever heard the phrase, "We have our lines crossed," or, "We don't have good lines of communication"? That is one of my favorite phrases because, whether we realize it or not, it describes the root of business troubles. In this section we will address how to strengthen these lines, or arrows, of communication between each of the Ways.

Way Ones—whether they are entrepreneurs or reside in enterprise—face the challenge of maintaining the vision, keeping the core principles, and looking outward. Sometimes they lose sight of the more immediate. They aren't always the best at figuring out how to develop a workable strategy that aligns with their business objectives and their vision. They can, however, sketch out a broad outline of the vision. The Way One can look at that outline and see the end result, but the strategy in between is blurry. This is why Way Ones depend so much on Way Twos to plan strategy and on Way Threes to implement and accomplish the tasks that the strategy requires.

We hear all the time that we need to "think outside of the box." What does that mean? An organization normally sets its business objectives for the year, develops strategies aligned to those objectives, and tactically implements them according to the plan. Then one day, someone introduces an idea, more than likely from the Way One. If this new idea is outside the scope of any tactical plan and you cannot directly tie it to a current business objective, then the idea is "outside the box." This constant tinkering fractures arrows between all Ways. ROE has defined the elusive "box."

IDEA ⇒ PLAN ⇒ ACTION

A concept that we have always assumed connotes creative brainstorming—thinking outside the box—is actually destructive in the realm of the business world. We need sound, actionable ideas. In my experience, a Way One will bombard his Way Twos (and Way Threes) with ideas when he feels that the current strategies are not producing the business results that he expected. Or perhaps there is a broken arrow or crossed lines of communication between the Way One and Way Two. It's then up to the Way Two to reign in the Way One's ideas and ask, "How can we implement a workable plan to achieve this vision?"

I recently had a Way Two come to me and say, "That's a great outside-the-box idea, but we have set the strategies that will accomplish this business objective, so can we see how the current strategy plays out first? If it doesn't produce the business results necessary, we will draw up a plan around that idea. Can we put that idea on the shelf and pull it out at the next business planning meeting?" Needless to say, we have a strong arrow between us. You might see this as semantics, "inside" or "outside" the box, but when communicating internally, this method draws the focus to the business objective and away from the constant randomness we experience every day. Randomness and confusion lead to broken arrows.

It also helps us process information at light speed in the twenty-first century. If we can file a great idea for later, it will make that next business planning session even more productive. Imagine everyone coming to the table with a list of outside-the-box ideas in their respective fields. What is distracting during the normal course of business tends to be exciting and motivating during these preplanned creative sessions. Rather, a good core value would be to look for the next "big idea." That would lead to a great ROE brainstorming meeting. Otherwise everyone will be unprepared for the meeting and the inevitable tinkering during the year will serve nothing more than to produce poor ROE and therefore poor ROI.

However, inside-the-box ideas—new ideas when the current ones are not working—or ideas that will make a group of tasks or strategy more efficient, thereby impacting ROE, are different. That inside-the-box idea can be tied to a current business objective (in other words, strong arrows in the division). Remember it's idea > plan > action *or* vision > strategy > tactic. If everyone has their own visual acuity then the ideas generated at each of the Ways of thinking will increase ROE. Those ideas should be celebrated.

Take the following example: I recently had a Way Three come to me and say, "I found an online file storage solution that could give us one hundred gigs of space for fifty dollars a year." Our existing solution was five gigabytes of space for one hundred dollars a year. Now, she was simply trying to get more storage for our clients' digital assets, but to me that idea was directly tied to a business objective: decrease fixed expenses by 10 percent. My response to her was, "You decreased the cost by 50 percent while increasing our capacity by twenty-fold. Great vision!" This is a great example of a Way Three thinker knowing how her daily tasks are tied to a business objective.

The vision is the far-reaching arc and trajectory established by the person sitting in the Way One seat. It is her responsibility to see it all, to see north, south, east, and west and all points in between. It is her responsibility to see not just what is, but what could be. It's important for the respective Way Three thinkers to explain how their role in the company ultimately impacts this vision. This means that the person in the Way Two seat has to understand both those in the Way Three seat and the one occupying the Way One seat. But they don't have the luxury of thinking in a Way One or a Way Three mode. If they do the former, they simply spin off into idea-land, where lots of great ideas get discussed but nothing gets done. If they do the latter, they end up micromanaging their Way Threes or taking the Way Three's seat and just doing the job themselves.

The same is true of any other position. Being a great Way Three doesn't mean they will also perform well as a Way Two. At the same time, it's important to recognize the qualities in your employees that may indicate that they would be a better fit in a different Way. For instance, there may be Way Threes who could be great Way Twos, but they are never mentored to think and communicate as Way Twos. A Way Three mind-set in a Way Two seat is a micromanager or an "I'll do it myself" manager, leaving little time to focus on planning. He's the manager who wants to be best friends with the Way Threes he should be managing. He's Michael Scott from *The Office*. No matter how much we love to watch him, none of us want to be him or have him working for—or managing—us.

Way Twos manage Way Threes by making sure the actions are performed according to plan. Also, they are on the lookout for Way Two thinking capabilities in their Way Threes. This will allow a Way Two to mentor their skills and characteristics to increase their own ROE and perhaps one day promote the Way Three. What is not measurable is not manageable. Accountability calls for a plan, a strategy, and now, as you know, a SMART plan.

One of the things I think a lot of companies fall into the trap of doing is that they could have a great idea or plan, but then it gets turned over to Way Threes without any input from them. It becomes meaningless. So it only helps if a Way Two develops the skill level of a Way Three by making them SMEs with their tools. Better plans, better execution, better business results, therefore high ROE and a greater return on investment. This input could have been a golden opportunity to pave the way to increased desire or, as we sometimes say, "buy-in" or "ownership." Passion is usually the highest at the Way One, but by opening the channel of communication (i.e., strengthening the arrows between the Ways), each employee becomes empowered and inspired to find their passion, too.

The Way Threes must have a strong arrow of communication between them. It's also critical that qualified Way Two managers manage the Way Threes by developing skill sets vital to the role. If this arrow is broken, it is usually the start of the process that ultimately leads the Way One to hyperactive idea mode because the original plan is not being tweaked frequently enough to produce the strategic plan results; thus it is missing the mark of the Way One's business goals.

A Way One in a mature organization who is busy within that organization is not being effective. The difference of working *in* (Way Two and Way Three functions) and not *on* (Way One functions related to vision) the business means he's being a Tasmanian devil. He needs to be out thinking of expanding frontiers. He needs to be out coming up with new ideas to be blended into the company vision or thinking outside the box. He does not need to be on the factory floor, managing the line. He needs to be thinking of the bigger picture.

Obviously this is less the case at a smaller company or one in its early stages, where the person who sits in the Way One chair also sits in one or more Way Two chairs as well, be it a Way Two of finance, Way Two of marketing, etc. The Way One is the driving force of the organization. They lead the people who write and manage the strategy who manage the people performing the tasks. The stage the business is in on the corporate life cycle will determine how often the Way One will need to change their thinking to a Way Two or Way Three role.

I experienced this myself when I formed my own advertising and promotional agencies. My vision was for both businesses to one day be vertically integrated and for me not to have to be involved in the day-to-day strategies and tactics. But in the beginning, I juggled all three seats until my company expanded and I was able to people-develop qualified successors for each role. It is important to change with this evolution, along with the vision crafted by a capable new Way One.

As tempting as it is for me to jump in at any Way of thinking, I do my best not to because I don't want to micromanage or tinker. Not only is it difficult to wear many hats in one organization, it is particularly difficult to wear many hats in multiple organizations.

That's not to say it can't be done. Think of the North American president of a global company based in Europe, or the head of a new generation nanotube division of a major high-tech manufacturer. For those within their aegis, they are the Way One. They set the vision so long as it aligns with the core organization's vision—thus they are Way Ones. But as soon as they get on that conference call to Bern or on that plane to the Portland headquarters, they are Way Two thinkers.

You can very well be the Way Two thinker over finance, but when looking just at the finance department within the context of a larger company, you are a Way One with a long-term vision as to how you see the department operating at optimal ROE. As soon as you step into the executive conference room, you are a Way Two thinker who must tie your strategies to the company's business objectives and communicate the business result impact of those strategies accordingly. What it comes down to is this: I would not be able to serve my clients or employees to the best of my abilities

> Great leaders communicate effectively and Return on Energy enhances communication effectiveness.

if I were a Way One of two companies and wearing all the hats of another. I can have all this going on around me because my ROE is high and my organization is powered by ROE.

A Way One has to understand sales, finance, operations, and all the other divisions that constitute his organization. He has to have that strong arrow between himself and his Way Twos, and know how the Way Twos should be communicating with the Way Threes. Great leaders communicate effectively and Return on Energy enhances communication effectiveness.

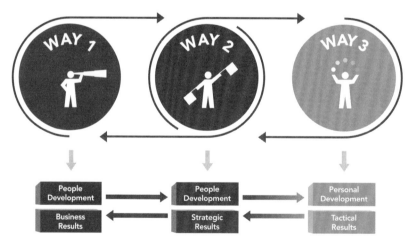

A client recently asked me if he could bounce an idea off me. We are both CEOs of our respective companies. I went into Way Two mode as soon as he said that, thinking of the arrow between us. I allowed him to fully explain his idea. I asked questions that were on point and not just curiosity questions. I provided feedback based upon my experience. He wanted to know if my team and I had the necessary experience to strategize and implement his idea.

The idea person needs someone to give her idea a sniff test. If they want to bounce an idea, they need a great Way Two who thinks how, not a great Way Three who thinks what. The arrow connecting the Way One to the Way Two shows how to put idea into action—that's Return on Energy, the right communication with the right person.

The Way Two then goes to the Way Three and finds out if an idea is doable. Again, the ideas are easy, but planning and implementation is another matter. If the Way One says, "Let's brainstorm," they mean to come to the table with one idea and leave with several ideas and no plan. But if the Way One says, "I'd like to bounce an idea off you," there will be one idea presented and a plan should be developed with a Way Three SME's input. If the meaning is not clarified or there is the wrong thinker in the wrong seat, then both parties will get frustrated—hence a broken arrow. This is grossly inefficient and a bad investment of time and effort, lowering everyone's ROE. A Way Three may not determine the strategy, but they should always have an understanding as to what it is so that they can better carry out the tactics and learn why they do what they do. Again, they are the what to the Way Two's how.

Now I plan to focus my ROE on my speaking and consulting business, and once again I find myself bouncing back and forth between each of the Ways. Just like any business start-up, I had an idea, crafted a vision, and now must write the plan and perform the tasks. Passion drives the process. And it's more important than ever for me to recognize the responsibilities of each of the Ways in order to achieve ROE within my new business. People with high levels of passion want to skip the planning phase and go from idea to action, but tactics without strategy—as you've learned—are a waste of money, and strategy without good tactical implementation is a waste of time.

When the newly hired Way Threes come aboard, they may or may not share that passion. If they do, that's great; if not, passion, like ideas, will overwhelm a Way Three thinker. Or perhaps one of the new Way Threes shares the passion and shows promise and is people-developed into a great Way Two. But in all my experience, a Way One cannot manage a Way Three thinker—unless that Way One reverts to a Way Two thinker and manages accordingly. Otherwise there is a breakdown in communication that leads to the Way Threes, if not everyone, becoming frustrated by this lack of cohesiveness. Way Threes need plans and roadmaps directing them to perform their tasks. Way Threes ultimately want to know why they are doing what they are doing. So, beyond the plan, they need a sense of purpose and management in order to make the plan workable.

Clearly defined and communicated strategies are what drive a Way Three's purpose. Plus it gives them a sense of mentorship when they are managed by someone who has their best interests in mind. And yet, Way Threes are often called upon to perform tactics, details, and actions without being informed as to how it fits into the strategy or the vision, hence a broken arrow between the Way Two and the Way Three. Managing them with vision and a high dose of passion, but without a Way Two to clearly communicate their strategy, is a slow death.

If an organization possesses the characteristics and skills but no mentoring or emphasis on people development, this will be their downfall. When a Way Two can communicate to the Way Three the reason for the task in a strong manner and the Way Three truly understands and aligns their tasks to that plan, ROE is going in the right direction. High ROE comes when results are generated at both the tactical and strategic level. Sometimes this communication style alone is enough for a Way Three to get the "aha" moment to become a more motivated, informed team member. As they say, a rising tide lifts all ships, and a low tide exposes holes. This people development process will impact the ROI of the business by using ROE. As you can see, there is a huge organizational benefit to having qualified Way Three thinkers in the Way Three seats.

Remember our example of Starbucks. They don't sell coffee. They sell community. They sell a place to come hang out. They sell a sense of welcome. Employee–customer interaction is their asset. They seem genuinely glad to see you. They take a personal interest in their regular customers. Their friendliness is not forced or phony. If they are acting, they are doing a great job. These are Way Threes who have a good arrow from and to the Way Twos, and who understand the strategy and the vision of the company. It is what makes you keep coming back for that five-dollar coffee drink.

And remember our Virgin Galactic mission to outer space. Any broken arrows of communication between Richard Branson, his team of directors, and his engineers and the rocket ship isn't getting past the ozone layer. There must be a clear vision of the task at hand in order to send their customers on a trip they'll never forget.

Ironically, the Way Two has to take charge. A Way Two is someone who can assert and challenge the Way One within

> The success of a start-up venture depends on a migration of thinking from idea to planning, to action, then to action delegation and planning delegation.

the confines of respect and etiquette. The Way Three is there to validate and say if it can be implemented, or to explain what tools they will need to make it happen because a Way Three is a SME. However, if after talking with a Way Three thinker, they can connect a task to a business objective, that would only mean the organization has strong arrows between the Ways and good people development.

The success of a start-up venture depends on a migration of thinking from idea to planning, to action, then to action delegation and planning delegation. If the right thinkers are put in the right seats during the recruiting process, then the founder will find herself in the Way One seat, truly thinking like a qualified Way One. This qualified Way One will continue to work on and refine her leadership skills, focusing on business results and people development while looking forward to make sure the vision remains clear. In turn, the Way Two will be able to receive this information, turn the vision into a workable strategy, and successfully manage their Way Threes to put the plan into action.

Going back to tourist flights into space—that has been an idea since the pulp science fiction novels in the 1930s. In 1968 they even showed commercial passenger space flight in Stanley Kubrick's *2001: A Space Odyssey*. But no one even considered it as a business model that could work until Virgin Galactic. Again, it took Sir Richard Branson to craft the idea into a vision, a team of people in Way Two seats to help him figure a way to make it feasible, and Way Three technicians to make extraterrestrial vacation a technical reality.

If the business has the privilege to progress to the next stage on the corporate life cycle by growing, then the question begs to be asked again: Do we have the right thinkers across all seats? The Way evaluation starts all over again. This is a major component of organizational development. And by employing ROE, you can prevent major issues later. The Way One is included in this comprehensive reevaluation in order to flourish at the next stage—usually the more profitable stage. How many founders of start-up companies remain Way Ones once the company grows into adolescence and ultimately adulthood? Start-up Way Ones thrive on the adrenaline of the start-up process. This is where ideas flow like water with unlimited boundaries, an idea typhoon. Many companies in later stages of development could benefit from the start-up-minded Way One thinker when their own innovation process hits the wall.

The communication arrow from Two to One has to be strong, and the message must be direct: "We are on plan." The Way Two then goes to the Way Three and finds out if an idea is doable, which in turn strengthens the arrow. Then ROE is high. When the arrow going back from Two to One is not strong, the Way One can overwhelm the Way Two. There is, then, a broken arrow, not a strong arrow.

Hence we use the ROE methodology to decipher the term "lines of communication." There is a time and place for brainstorming, sharing ideas, and thinking outside the box, but not in the middle of plan implementation—unless a course-correction is necessary, meaning the plan is not producing the desired strategic or business result. That's ROE. That's a series of strong arrows connecting the Ways. And that's how it can affect your ROI. ROE powers ROI.

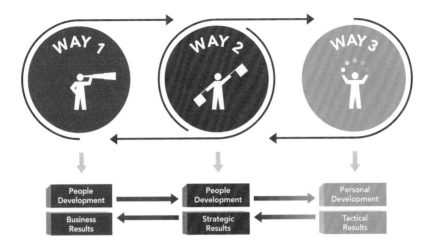

See how this comes together?

It's an entirely different way of thinking and seeing things, but it's so intuitive you'll be surprised that it's been right in front of you all along.

SECTION IV

The CEO Sits in the Bull's-Eye

seven

The ROE Organizational Chart

The achievements of an organization are the results
of the combined effort of each individual.
—Vince Lombardi

We need to fundamentally change how people view the classic organizational chart. The classical org chart is rooted in a style of management from the time when calculations were done on hand-cranked adding machines and our country was connected by railroads and steam locomotives. In so many ways, business has evolved, but the org chart—with its early-twentieth-century, top-down, hierarchical perspective—is one thing that still devils even the most forward-thinking, Six Sigma–devoted business organizations.

There is a better way.

When we look at this chart we have to keep in mind that we are talking about changing a pure fundamental, so if it seems like the terminology is simple, that's like saying that talking about proteins as a building block of life is simple. We want this to be accessible to anyone, regardless of his or her background. What we are trying to do is to fit this new, round peg into the space where the old square hole of an org chart was. So don't just gloss over the terminology here—each word is offered with significant meaning.

Let's review what we've learned so far: ROE is the traditional organizational chart on its side—not top down, but side to side. It all starts with the vision triangle and the positioning of the Ways.

The vision triangle extends from the Way One onward.

The Way One is surrounded by his closest advisors.

Let's combine these charts and create something new: an objective is a target. A target is most commonly associated with a bull's-eye. And in the case of ROE, the target in the middle represents the business objectives set by the Way One.

How is your vision tied to measurable and manageable key business objectives? What SMART strategic plans are tied to those objectives, and furthermore, are the thousands of tactics performed every day connected to the business objectives through the strategic plan? Are there qualified thinkers managing each step in the communication chain tied to their desired results? From the center, the bull's-eye is a line of communication from Way One to Way Two to Way Three and, of course, back again. This line of communication, or spoke of a division, is repeated for as many divisions that exist. And that's the basic model for how lines of communication and responsibility work within the ROE organizational chart.

At the center—the bull's-eye—is the person in the hot seat. This is the Way One. The immediate ring around the Way One is the organization's Way Twos. These are the heads of divisions such as marketing, sales, operations, finance, human resources, and all the other functions of a modern business enterprise, regardless of the field or industry. Everything in business somehow impacts something else, whether or not it's directly related—like how "the cost of goods sold" expense on the income statement is related to inventory on the balance sheet. You can now start to actually see from the ROE organizational chart the critical role each of the Ways occupies in these casual connections. Now it should start to become apparent that the Way One is actually in the center, flanked by her closest advisors, the qualified Way Two thinkers from each corporate division.

The Way Two is responsible for communicating with the Way One and managing his Way Threes, but there is also a relationship within the team of Way Twos—the direct reports. These relationships occur obviously from a personnel perspective, but also from a plan perspective. How is sales related to marketing, or finance related to operations? When qualified Way Twos get together with their individual areas of subject matter expertise they bring to the table how their plans are aligned to common business

> The Ways must keep pace with the development of the organization.

objectives. This puts a new emphasis on a strategic team meeting, a corporate retreat, or the executive team.

Furthermore, just like a person is never in a static state of one Way of thinking or another, the organization itself does not exist in a static state. The organization therefore will be developed if the Ways practice Return on Energy to achieve their own, and the organization's, shared goals. The Ways must keep pace with the development of the organization. This is the same as the preventive health measure we take for our personal well-being. We can save ourselves a lot of time and money, not to mention live a longer and happier life, if we just enforce discipline in our daily activities. This is the same hope we have for our organizations.

I once spoke to a chief operating officer of a company that services the airline industry. She told me that after many attempts at strategic retreats during which they would outline the "strategic plan" for the upcoming year with many great ideas from the executive team, they could not get total buy-in from the company when they returned. So they adopted a method called strategic deployment.

Going back to chapter 1, sometimes we miss the most obvious things in our quest for unnecessary complexity. Sometimes the self-evident gets buried under so much meaningless jargon and so many business buzzwords that we don't see how we're talking right past each other and not connecting at all.

Let's use ROE to decipher "strategic deployment." Therefore let's take "daily control activities" to mean tasks; "need to link" to mean the arrows from Way Three to Way Two and back again; and "company strategy," if communicated well by the Way Two and thus implying a strong arrow, to mean managing by explaining why the Way Three thinker is doing what they are doing. Lost in these indecipherable buzzwords, the best, most life-altering, game-changing ideas would simply and immediately die upon contact.

Going back to the target, the outer ring is comprised of the Way Three thinkers. They are the gatekeepers and the company's front line. We move into an area where job titles are often defined as verbs rather than nouns. They are the people with whom customers and clients most often deal. They are the face of the organization as much as the Way One. They are gatekeepers, like the membrane of the cell, protecting it from harm but allowing in what will keep it alive and well. The cell membrane will only remain alive and well because, like the parts of the cell, they all need to function properly individually so as a whole it can thrive.

The number of people in an organization grows from the single Way One to the number of Way Twos to the number of Way Threes. Is a company top-heavy or too left side–heavy? Are there too many Way One thinkers and not enough people who understand how to take an idea to action? There is only one CEO, only one Way One. There is only one vision for the core company. Competing visions will eventually collide. The collision will sometimes produce competition. Remember, vision refers to core values, core purpose, and the mission of the organization. If anyone on the organizational chart sees a different vision from the core vision, they will either go with someone who shares that philosophy and mentor them or venture out into the new frontier on their own.

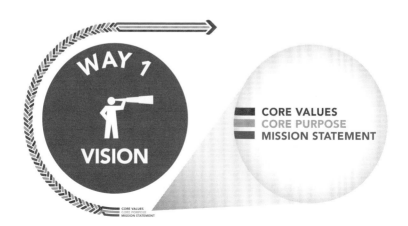

WAY 1
VISION

CORE VALUES
CORE PURPOSE
MISSION STATEMENT

The Way Twos and Way Threes break out like slices of pie. Or, if you've ever visited a pub, you may notice that it looks like the segments of a dartboard with the Way Twos and Way Threes in their respective segments. Guess who everyone wants to hit with a dart? With the communication delivery chain moving from Way One to Two to Three and back again, we get even more egalitarian and less hierarchical. We turn the old top-down model on its side, both literally and figuratively. And as we have described, the Way One possesses the vision. The vision originates from a single point that must blanket the entire organization.

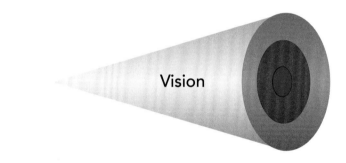

That's why we call Way Twos the vision amplifiers, the VPs of Vision to thrust the force of vision. The fuel for thrust is passion. You can also imagine the vision triangle as a megaphone, with the Way Two chanting like Ty Pennington on the bullhorn, "OK, folks! This is the vision; these are the business objectives and strategic plans! This is the mission and core values that will guide us to success!"

Rarely does anyone in an organization have more passion than the Way One, especially the entrepreneurial Way One. So when you couple the passion of the Way One and her leadership characteristics, you then have qualified Way Twos ready to manage the plan by managing people, not tasks. But again, if a Way Two is doing the task then they are not managing and not thinking like a Way Two, but like a Way Three.

However, what would happen if a Way One could build a company or a division that possessed an equal level of passion—or more? What would that passion curve look like? Observe this chart: some would say that the red arrow is typical with high passion on the Way One side and progressively less moving from Two to Three. Maybe the management team is strong and the passion curve looks something like the green arrow. I think the goal of every Way One, regardless of the exit strategy, is to accomplish the purple arrow, but the Way One privately dreams of the orange arrow, wondering if he has the mentorship skills, leadership skills, and characteristics to one day wake to this reality.

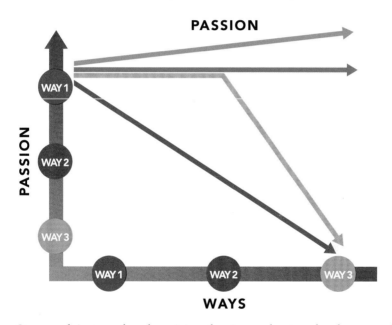

Our goal is to take the vision horizontal triangle shape and complete the organizational chart by aligning the points together until we complete the organizational divisions to complete the circle, like a game of pick-up sticks where the sticks fall into a perfect sphere.

Everyone in the organization should have vision or ideas, not just the Way One. We cannot break away from long-held beliefs too quickly. After all, it's taken decades to cement the traditional organizational chart into our minds with operations starting with construction of the railroads. Business is a hierarchy, and

> Ideas only come from people.

many are climbing the corporate ladder to get to the next rung. This is one of the few examples in the ROE methodology where we use a top-down, bottom-up model to demonstrate a point, because ideas only come from people, and if we can somehow focus great ideas to the three Ways of thinking, collectively we can move mountains.

I explain it like this: The Way One is sitting at the top of the vision triangle. His vision at the top is 360 degrees; he can see in all directions—to the north, the south, the west, the east, and all points between them. Hence he has complete vision, but it is more of a farsighted type of vision (i.e., he can see clearly in the distance, but sometimes not so well with what's right in front of him).

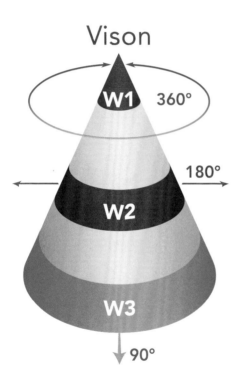

Vison

W1 360°

180°

W2

W3

90°

A Way Two may sit on the north face and can see 180 degrees, due east and west, with some points between with limited peripheral vision. If this Way Two would communicate with the Way Two on the east face they could see together more broadly. The Way One's team of Way Twos (direct reports) should have a combined vision of the Way One and collectively align their plans to the business objectives of the company. This is the reason for executive boardroom meetings or the long days spent at off-site strategic retreats.

Some of the best inside-the-box ideas may come from qualified Way Threes—the SMEs with their tools, the ones who can see with a laser-like focus that amazes most Way Twos and Ones with a new and efficient way of doing something (the operative word being "doing"). The Way Three thinkers are more nearsighted (i.e., they can see what is right in front of them with little or no assistance or distractions), but the corrective lenses of the Way Two and One are necessary to see what is in the distance. Therefore the Way Threes can see 90 degrees or straight ahead with some points to the right and left, but with more limited peripheral vision.

Consider the game "Telephone" that we played as kids. One person started a story and then it was carried around a circle to see if the facts remained the same all the way to the last person. Often times, the result was that the end story was far different from the original message. The Way Twos must be keepers of the story, amplifiers of the vision, managers of the business objectives with their strategies, and keepers of the passion.

When you take the vision triangle and show how it relates between Way One, Two, and Three thinkers, you start to see how it ties in to the different perspectives among the Ways. But you never know from which vantage point the next big idea is going to come. This is why I like to get weigh-in on strategic plans from Way Threes who are SMEs with the tools that will be used to execute the plan.

To reiterate: the Way Ones maintain the 360-degree vision, the Way Twos work with a 180-degree view, and the Way Threes keep a sharp eye out straight ahead and see with most detail. The vision triangle takes on the shape of a three-dimensional cone and ultimately the organizational chart of Return on Energy.

Build up from there with the ROE methodology and it all starts to come together. We'll also use it to illustrate what happens when you have broken arrows where you should have strong arrows, and what happens when you have a Way Two thinker or a Way Three thinker in the wrong place. A Way Three thinker in a Way Two seat will not be able to adequately manage, much less mentor, Way Threes by building successful strategies tied to business objectives while also effectively communicating with the Way Twos in adjacent divisions of the company and with his Way One. A Way Three thinker in a Way Two seat will be thinking what rather than how.

Likewise, if a Way Two thinker is in a Way Three seat or a Way Two or Three thinker is in a Way One seat, they are only set up for failure—or at the very least, poor ROE and a compromised ROI. Organizational development experts are called to spin the wheel and essentially settle the right qualified thinkers in the proper seats.

Understanding this framework for ROE methodology is a big step in seeing something that has been right in front of you the whole time. The most critical thing to consider is that the ROE organizational chart is created for a new way of thinking about business, the people in it, and their desired results. It is an illustration of the labor force—the actual force of labor an organized body of people can bring to bear. Not force in the brute sense, but force in terms of intellectual, client or customer service, and market strength. Ideation is a powerful force in life and when ROE is high, ideation is high, so let's go move that mountain.

We use these new paradigms to help us make an organization's communications and efforts work more efficiently and to connect the right person to the right result. We all want to work smarter, not harder. That's ROE.

So how do we do it?

You may think that most companies and organizational structures are much more complex than the simplicity of the three Ways. Obviously it's not as simple as one Way One, one Way Two, and a team of Way Threes in one division. In an effort to keep its simplicity and resist the pitfalls of complexity, I have found that sticking with this structure is the most effective. But in doing so, you have to know how and when to shift the communication chain and ROE organizational chart when the situation calls for it. Is Jerry Jones the Way One of the Dallas Cowboys? Of course, but in the context of the NFL, Roger Goodell, the NFL commissioner, is the Way One.

I recently worked with a client we will call Elliott, who reported to the COO and had three direct reports that had a combined staff of about fifteen people. Elliott's division was responsible for three revenue drivers of the company. Now in this scenario, the COO is the Way Two, right? Elliot is a Way Two and his direct reports are Way Twos also, right? Well, what happens when you take Elliott out of the bigger picture and set him up at the point of the vision triangle of his own division?

In other words, remove a slice of pie and put it on its own plate. Elliott becomes the Way One thinker and his direct reports become the Way Twos and this "division" becomes its own pie with three slices. I asked him, "What is your vision for your department? Where do you want to be in five years? What are your business objectives that will be help you accomplish this?"

Was I talking to him as a Way Two or Way One? Right, Way One. Then we shifted to the parent organization of his division. We talked about the organization as a whole business, then we aligned his new divisional business objectives with the organizational business objectives while maintaining common vision between them. When he met with his supervisor, the COO of the organization, he presented him with the way in which the departmental vision was aligned to the organizational vision. He presented with passion how his business objectives, along with the strategies his direct reports were managing, were aligned to the department objectives and how his direct reports were managing the people who were performing the critical tasks.

What did Elliott present to his COO? Simply put, a strategy, but the strategy was a child-type company organizational structure within the parent company. We just approached it like it was its own business unit. The benefit of this exercise was twofold. First, Elliott was able to design a well-thought-out SMART strategy that was powered by ROE. Since Elliot's work method was now powered by ROE, he was able to connect the right person with the right result. This included himself knowing when to lead, manage, or be the action officer. Elliott clearly has the characteristics to develop himself while developing his people, but not development for development's sake. Second, this exercise was the same practice for running a company as a whole or mentoring him to one day become a qualified Way One thinker. So was Elliott a Way One, Two, or Three thinker?

He must be all of them, but thinking the proper way at the proper times. Elliott was disciplined enough not to spin off into idea-land when the situation called for laser-like focus and so on. At the end of the meeting with the COO, he of course tied his departmental vision to the COO's strategic objectives, which were accordingly tied to the CEO's business objectives.

During the course of working with him he showed me an article sitting on his desk: "Best Practices for Managing Yourself, Managing Others, and Managing Your Business." Elliott reread the article with the Return on Energy methodology in mind and was able to have a clearer understanding of the subject matter and the valuable concepts he could employ. Did the subject matter change? Of course not—his perception changed due to an increased awareness. It was right

> ROE is the tool that will make all your other tools work better.

in front of him the entire time. I am glad that the ROE method is being applied to enhance the understanding of other subject matter. ROE is the tool that will make all your other tools work better.

Therefore, ROE is not designed to compete with other leadership, management, communications, business, or personal development methods, but rather to enhance the understanding of them, making them work better. Do you think that Elliott, armed with the ROE awareness and his experiences, will make a great CEO one day? You bet. The ROE organizational chart was a beneficial tool to navigate around from the parent and child organizations and to know when to think and communicate like a One, Two, or Three.

SECTION V

Connect the Right People in the Right Way

eight

Way One Communication: "The Bigger Picture"

People ask the difference between a leader and a boss.
The leader leads, and the boss drives.

—Theodore Roosevelt

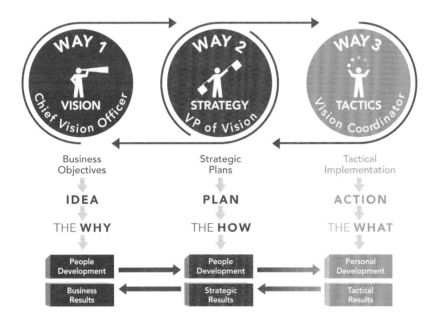

I've now introduced you to Way One, Way Two, and Way Three, respectively. In the next three chapters, we'll go deeper into the three Ways, describing how different thinkers can increase their productivity in order to increase ROE. I want to talk about how you and your organization can be powered by Return on Energy. We will accomplish this by laying out a framework for how they interact. The Way is a new word in business, but the methodology has been in front of you the whole time. We are just providing a new perspective—just like the ROE in this book's logo.

I want to continue driving home the message that a Way is not a permanent position or state of mind. But by thinking in one Way or another and having a degree of awareness of the type of thinking of the person with whom you communicate, you will establish a strong arrow between the two of you—strong lines of communication.

Throughout the course of the day, I think like a Way One, Two, and Three. I have to if I am going to relate to people. I have an imaginary three-sided apparatus on my desk and whatever side is facing me is the Way I should be thinking and communicating at that moment in time. Likewise, I pay close attention to whomever I am speaking with to make sure I am establishing a strong arrow between us. I think one of the mistakes we tend to make when communicating with people at work is that, through the course of the conversation, we are trying so hard to get our point across and get what we want that we fail to look at the conversation from the other person's perspective. Challenge yourself by asking: How are they processing the information? How do they think? This exercise gets particularly fun in a group setting or networking group.

Next time you find yourself among a group of people, sit back and observe. I begin by asking myself, "Am I speaking to a Way Two thinker here or a Way Three?" I know their job title is marketing coordinator, but they sure do speak strategic lingo. Once you identify their Way of thinking, then you can connect them to their desired result. What happens if the person with whom you are conversing does the same thing? Yes, that's right— both of your needs will get met because you both will work on connecting each other to your respective desired results.

I use this methodology all the time. For example, several years ago we found ourselves in a request for proposal process. We found out that we were one of twelve agencies being considered to rebrand a high-profile business in the community. We also found out that not only were we one of twelve, but all our competition had creative portfolios in this space and we did not. Furthermore, the prospect had looked at over seventy-five logos over a five-year period. My team wanted this one.

Return on Energy was our biggest weapon. We knew if we connected the right people to their desired results, we not only would have a higher margin of victory, but it would prove that ROE is a valid methodology to deliver value.

In our first meeting, the president addressed the brand, the colors, and many of the details that go into the brand, but not the vision. We simply asked "visionary" questions: Where do you see the business in five or ten years? What do you see your clientele looking like in ten years? We talked about core values, purpose, and mission. We explained that the purpose is the guiding star of the business, a very far-out goal that might be reached in one hundred years. We talked about mission and the mountain range we must traverse on our path, our Way, to the star—the purpose. It might take us ten years to traverse this mountain, and on the other side of that mountain is another mountain where we will set another mission. The core values will be the compass guiding us to stay on the path (the Way) and not get lost and wind up on the wrong mountain range. The values, mission, and purpose make up the vision. We need to build a brand for the future state of the organization.

The president started to tell us what she saw. She was now looking out to the future from the mountaintop, not at the base camp. What she saw was the future, her vision. We simply spoke to her as a Way One—not as any other Way—and coached Way One responses. She had the brand in her head; we just needed to get her communicating like a Way One and then put it on paper for her. During this process, her staff, her Way Twos and Threes, was present. We connected the Twos to the business development strategy of the business and how a new and exciting brand will enhance the strategic results of the business development and marketing campaigns. We connected the Way Threes to the tactical implementation of a new brand rollout within a company and the ease of redoing letterhead, signage, and business cards. We addressed their anxiety at having to put more on their already-full plates; we talked implementation, execution—action. Once we connected each meeting member—each influencer—to their desired result, we had all the information we needed to position ourselves as "the agency that gets us," then prepare and pitch our ideas.

Pitch day was exciting because we were prepared. They paraded agencies in and out every thirty or so minutes. We pitched three brand ideas. During the brand pitch we reconnected each Way to their desired result (whether they knew it as their result or not) with a story of what the future could look like with this brand and how it would impact them individually. At the end of the pitch, the CEO sat back and said, "In thirty years, this was the most exciting marketing meeting I have ever been involved in." They chose the very first brand we presented—the one the president saw in her vision. They turned out to be a great client because we positioned ourselves as trusted advisors using ROE, and they saw the value we brought beyond our core deliverables for which they paid.

ROE was a success yet again.

I use ROE outside of the office all the time, too. One day I walked into a new local health foods store. The store concept is providing prepared, good-for-you meals that can be heated up in the store or at home. As soon as I walked in, a person introduced himself as Jim. I made pleasantries and found out Jim was the store manager. I knew that Jim, being a Way Two, was someone who was more than likely responsible for creating and making sure there are strong strategic results for the store and the company as a whole.

I told him that I saw the flier displayed in my gym and that prompted me to come into the store, hence the desired strategic result of the flier strategy. I complimented him on the store's location and reinforced that it was in a highly health-conscious community. I then asked if someone could share the details of the store's concept with me. I knew full well that he was more than capable of doing it, but I wanted to learn more specifics from a Way Three thinker and gauge their level of passion. The manager introduced me to an associate who, with great passion, explained to me the prepared-meal concept, the nutritional content of the food, the quality of ingredients, and so on.

Then, using his iPhone, he showed me a picture of himself from a year ago, showing me that he had lost almost forty pounds with their meal concept. I asked pretty detailed questions, from the food ingredients to the macronutrient breakdown of each meal. I was convinced he was a subject matter expert in his field with a high level of passion—the kind of Way Three thinker every Way One hopes for.

I purchased my meals from a very friendly person at the checkout who was very efficient with the cash register, was paying close attention to how my meals were bagged, and actually walked around the counter to hand me my purchase and thank me with a smile. As I walked out I saw who I suspected was the Way One and told him that he had a great, passionate, and knowledgeable staff, and that I loved his concept. I wanted to connect him to his desired result—people development and business results—so I told him those magic words: "I'll be back."

In the outdated, hierarchical organization chart that was established in the last century, Way Ones are at the top of the page, Way Twos in the middle, and Way Threes are at the bottom. The first thing you have to do is think differently about the position of each seat on the abstract chart. I like to think in terms of left and right—side to side rather than up and down.

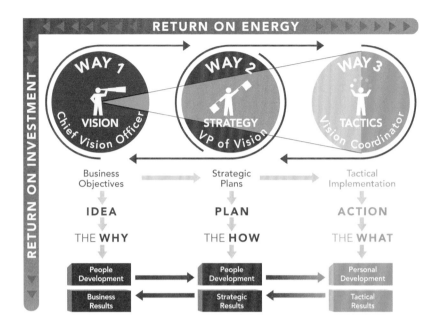

In reality, the lines of communication connected with arrows are horizontal, like power lines on power poles. No power can be transmitted if the lines are down. Way Ones on the left, Way Twos in the middle, and Way Threes on the right. Where does the president of the United States sit during the cabinet meetings? If you have ever watched Donald Trump's show, *The Apprentice*, where does The Donald sit in the boardroom? They both sit in the middle, flanked by their Way Twos, with higher-ranking officers sitting closer to the center of the table. If you were to look at the center of the table going either to the right or left, the order would be Way One, Way Twos, and Way Threes.

This order is very important because those closest in proximity to the center are also the closest advisors to the Way One. In the legend of King Arthur's round table, the table was a place where the king's knights, his closest advisors, congregated before battle to get instructions from the King. Some historians believe that there was no actual table, just a circular meeting space with regional noblemen in the front row and lower-ranked subjects grouped around the outside of the circle. This arrangement was symbolic: a round table, after all, has no head. In this circle of communication, every person's opinion was just as important as everyone else seated around the circle. The lines of communication go back and forth, not up and down. Ideally, they flow from One to Two, Two to One, Two to Three, Three to Two, and back from Two to One. Like the knights of the round table, let's open the lines of communication.

Take those basic ideas of vision, strategy, and tactics and see how they align left to right, going from a narrow tunnel of vision to a broad, focused beam of energy—action in motion.

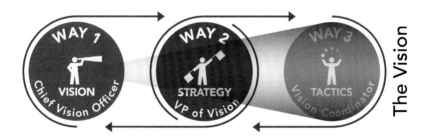

So far we've talked about some of the basic things that go into a Way One thinker's makeup: they are passionate, they have vision, and they think abstractly but with coherent reason. But there are other characteristics necessary to occupy that Way One seat. Way Ones have to have good interpersonal skills. They have to be able to speak to people from across the spectrum of society—investors, directors, peers, community leaders, managers, employees, and even the ordinary person on the street.

Being able to deal with and understand people from end-users to their competitors feeds Way Ones' inspiration for perceiving a new—or better—product or service. For example, if a Way One is passionate about exemplary customer service, you bet she will have customer service ideas. Her Way Two who is responsible for customer service will need to have her game on each and every day.

Way Ones are also motivated, and they are problem solvers. They can take an initial idea and draw out the broad strokes for a plan on a sheet of scratch paper or a whiteboard; they might even use mind map applications. What they put down isn't necessarily detailed, and it isn't complete, but it is the rough idea of how to take a vision to action when looking at it from—as the saying goes—forty thousand feet. Legend has it that Herb Kelleher drew out the vision of Southwest Airlines on the back of a napkin.

A Way One sets the vision, but their skill is in mentoring and leading people, not managing people. Leading and managing are two very different things, and most people don't understand the wide gulf. Leadership is a product of vision; management is a product of strategy. It is important to consider both the short-term and long-term health of the organization. Leaders think outside the box and come up with big ideas that lead to innovation, while managers must have the nearsightedness to create strategies that can implement the innovations that will accomplish the vision. I stress this again: ideas without plans are pipe dreams. The plans must be SMART plans.

> Ideas without plans are pipe dreams.

Leaders have a charismatic and transformational style. Some leaders can also fill the role of manager, but most managers are not leaders. This is a very important distinction. Leaders can fill the role as managers. Translation: a qualified Way One can also think like a Way Two when called upon, but it's not their best and highest use. However, this distinction is not a two-way street: most managers are not leaders.

It comes down to people development. Most Way Twos have not been mentored enough to think like a Way One, much less to be a qualified Way One. Therefore, when identifying a CEO or president as a Way One thinker, sometimes (but not always) it's implied that they can also think like a Way Two.

Leaders are risk-seekers, and they inspire people to rise to the occasion. Leaders are focused on achievement. Managers, meanwhile, have larger teams. They seek to maximize outcomes while minimizing risk. They are process-oriented and focused on transactions and producing results—both strategic results and business results to which the strategy is tied. They have numerous control measures that they can read like the dials and gauges in an airliner cockpit. Way Ones mentor and lead the people managing the plans who manage the people doing the work.

When you "bounce an idea" off a Way Three, they are waiting for the plan, not more ideas. Qualified Way Twos are the people off whom you can bounce an idea, and Way Threes will verify if it can or cannot be done or if it is implementable. A Way Three usually already has a lot on their plate and more ideas may only increase their anxiety level. In this situation the Way One will get bothered because after all, it's a great big idea! The Way One starts having the conversation in their head, "Why can't anyone see that this is a game-changing idea?" Whereas if this conversation had occurred with a qualified Way Two, the Way Two would know that his role is to receive this big idea, ask himself, "Is this an inside- or outside-the-box idea?" and start the gifted way of thinking and planning.

A Way Two will ask themselves, "Is this idea even possible?" The answer to this question is usually, "No way," but the Way Two should sketch a rough plan and collect information from a group of Way Three thinkers with subject matter expertise and the tools and tasks involved in the plan. Just like the trap the Way One falls into by going to a Way Three or a Way Three thinker in a Way Two seat, the Way Two cannot go to an unmotivated Way Three for subject matter expertise input. Only people can generate ideas, and ideas lead to innovation, whether it is the invention of the assembly line, Pong, or Post-it Notes.

> Only people can generate ideas, and ideas lead to innovation.

The same applies to brainstorming. Anyone can participate in brainstorming, where all thinkers can come together to produce many ideas originating from one. However, an idea has a higher probability that it can be taken to action when the room is Way thinker–balanced as opposed to everyone thinking in the same Way.

I want to emphasize that a Way might be a position, but it is also a Way of thinking. You could have the title of CEO (Way One) but routinely think a totally different Way, which actually indicates that you may be unqualified for that seat. Adversely, if a qualified Way One is communicating with an unqualified Way Two, then they are going to run into challenges in creating a strategy—or in other words, have a broken arrow. In this case, it's time to return to the ROE infographic to determine how to fix this broken arrow. Maybe it's a simple matter of changing seats or adapting to a different Way of thinking and means to connect the Ways to their desired results. Return on Energy allows for people to disagree or resolve these broken arrows without being disagreeable.

nine

Way Two Communication: "The Big Picture"

Details create the big picture.
—Sanford I. Weill

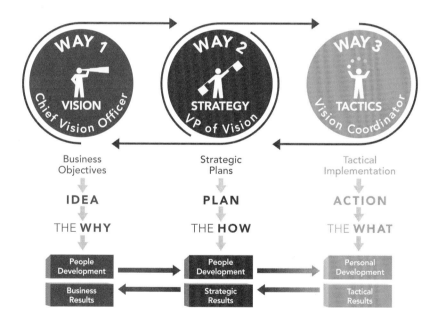

Aqualified Way Two will want to learn the economics of the business as a whole, not just their piece of the organizational pie. Why does a company do what it does? What are its business models? How does it make money? How does marketing work in relation to operations or manufacturing? What is the relationship between sales and marketing, as seen by other departments and between the two? They are great managers of the corporate strategic retreat. They take the vision like a megaphone and amplify it throughout their areas of the organization.

The ideal Way Two can also analyze problems without getting lost in analysis. They can understand the implications of potential trade-offs of all kinds, including the trade-off between acting sooner with less information and later with more.

A Way Two can develop a plan that is made up of many complex tasks, and managing it requires their own tasks—budgeting, creating a timeline, delegation, and creating metrics to measure progress. And a Way Two may be managing many plans at once. They understand that what is not measurable is not manageable. So they have to be systematic thinkers. They are juggling many balls, but unlike the Way Three who also juggles, the Way Two juggles strategies, not tasks.

Business Objectives → **Strategic Plans** → Tactical Implementation

An ideal Way Two can push back against a Way One, whether it's in bringing a flight of ideas under control or explaining why an idea is not implementable as it was conceived.

Way Twos have to determine how to plan, develop the plan, identify deliverables, estimate time and cost, create metrics and controls, create a way to track progress, determine who is going to do what, develop the schedule and budget, and then manage the implementation of the plan, which has its own lengthy task list. Whereas Way Threes are SMEs with their tools, Way Twos are SMEs of the industry. When a Way Two hears a new idea, they think that the plan may need to be reorganized and reprioritized, and since they like order, this can be a stressful proposition.

Ultimately, it's about the plan. A Way Two has to know how to write a plan, document a plan, and then empower, influence, and manage the Way Threes to accomplish the tasks needed to achieve the plan's goals. They keep focus on the *bigger* picture—the Way One's vantage point—while getting Way Threes to see the big picture—the Way Three and Two's vantage points. At the end of the day, Way Twos manage results.

BIG PICTURE

BIGGER PICTURE

Way Two thinkers should always resist the urge just to jump in and do it themselves. Action items, tasks, the small incremental steps necessary to complete a project will beckon them. If a Way Two is managing an unmotivated Way Three thinker, then the urge will only be intensified. If this is the case then we are dealing with broken arrows where ROE is low.

If a Way Two is involved in the implementation of the tasks, how can they truly keep sight on the critical results of the big picture? How can they manage the strategic results in order to keep the plan successfully moving forward? Remember, some of the

> Qualified Way Twos will know that they manage people, not tasks.

sweetest words to a Way One's ears are from the Way Two: "We are on plan." People development is critical to achieving this— mentor and manage. Qualified Way Twos will know that they manage people, not tasks. However, in smaller organizations, the Way Two must sometimes be the Way Three. If this is the case, when it calls for the Way Two to think like a Way Three, they must really focus and nail the part.

The same applies to micromanaging, which usually occurs when there is a Way Three thinker in a Way Two seat. Micromanagers are tacticians, and tacticians are Way Threes. Tacticians maneuver to achieve a particular short-term aim. A true manager, a qualified Way Two, should be focusing on more long-term aims. Otherwise how would they even begin to establish a strong arrow to the Way One? Not to mention a strong arrow to the Way Threes—otherwise the Threes will never learn the necessary skills and understand why they are doing what they are doing. Skills build confidence, but not just self-confidence—confidence in the mentor–mentee relationship, hence a strong arrow. Therefore a qualified Way Two is also a skill builder, a confidence builder, and a results collector. That's why strategic results are connected to business results and people development. When the Way Three understands the how to their what, they then can see the big picture. The Way Two lives in the big picture format, but his Way One is always trying to get the Way Two to see the bigger picture. And with the speed of innovation, the bigger picture is like a high-definition, three-dimensional, one hundred–inch television screen.

One of my clients graduated in the top of his class from an Ivy League school with a graduate degree and took a job in a Way Two seat. Is he a micromanager or an I-will-just-do-it-myself manager? No. He relies heavily on a team of Way Threes to perform the tasks necessary to accomplish the goals of his plans. He has a tendency to overlook the level of detail, the laser-like focus, and the endless task juggling necessary to keep his plans on track, and he could not survive without his team of people. That doesn't mean he's not a great mentor to his Way Threes; in this case, however, his skills—a collection of invaluable experiences—are ahead of the organizational development curve and even ahead of the vision.

So either the company growth needs to catch up to his skill level or he will need to learn Way Three skills sets until that growth happens.

Basically every communication between a Way One and a Way Two should be tied to the business objective. Everything else is a distraction or is outside the box. That's where the skill of leadership in the Way One comes into play. They have to set expectations and hold managers accountable for ensuring that their goals are met—but more times than not, they are actually preventing progress with constant idea sharing or tinkering due to the high passion levels.

Sometimes, of course, it falls on the Way Twos to hold the Way One accountable. Suppose a Way One has set four objectives: increase yearly sales by 30 percent, bring the skill level up on all Way Threes in the company, decrease fixed costs by 10 percent, and increase the gross profit margin by 5 percent on average. The Way One may not realize that taken as a whole, these objectives require the acquisition of new office space. If the Two is qualified, she can push back and explain how the Two needs to add "new office space" to the strategy list because it's something that is tied to the other four, and it is something that needs its own plan as surely as any other operational objective. With this adjustment, they can then report back to the Way One with the sweetest words any Way One could hear: "We are on plan."

I once taught a class of college seniors. After the class a student told me she was having trouble deciding on a job offer and asked if we could use ROE to analyze the situation. The job title she was interviewing for was director of marketing. The job duties involved many tasks that were not tied to any identifiable plan. The CEO of the company interviewed her, and ultimately he was the one who offered her the job. His passion during the interview process was very high and he shared many of his ideas that related to marketing. She asked what she should do. I asked if she was going to get two paychecks. She said, "What do you mean?"

"Well," I told her, "you are being hired to be a Way Three, but you will be in a Way Two role in the eyes of the Way One." Since there was no one to whom she could delegate and she had never developed marketing strategies, much less managed people, she felt like she was being set up for failure. She called me several months later and told me she had turned down the job offer and took a job as a Way Three in order to hone her skills in an area where she really wanted to concentrate on being a SME. Before I could even ask the question, she told me, "Yes, my manager is a qualified Way Two. I determined that during my interview." Because she understood the importance of ROE and the different Ways of thinking, my student was able to find a job that was not only a good fit, but also utilized her skills and offered the potential for growth in the future.

ten

Way Three Communication

The people who are doing the work are the moving force behind the Macintosh. My job is to create a space for them, to clear out the rest of the organization and keep it at bay.
—Steve Jobs

Way Threes may have some or all aspects of the other Ways, but in different measure or focus. Ideally, a person in a Way Three seat has the potential to one day fill any seat. But they start with basics, like being good team players. Way Threes by definition have to be good team players. They want their team to look good and are willing to share what they know to help their peers because they see how their work goes into the larger effort. They see how their tasks fit into the plan, which is designed to accomplish the overall business objective of the company.

A motivated Way Three demonstrates accountability and integrity, is trustworthy, and honors commitments. He is resilient and overcomes setbacks. He is respectful of his peers and those in other seats in the organization. He works to build constructive relationships to the benefit of the organization, not just himself. He is good at taking verbal directions and can prioritize and adapt to changes. He is a SME who becomes a master of the tools he uses—be those tools microscopes, ratchets, customer service skills, fiber optics, or train engines.

But there's more. He is willing to accept challenges from others and from himself. He is fundamentally curious about the product or products of your company or group. If he doesn't have a fascination with the product or service, he isn't becoming the SME that his position demands. If he deals with customers, he won't be able to have engaging conversations about the product or service if he only knows it from a script.

An ideal Way Three should maintain the same type of long-term approach that a good company does. Way Threes need to focus on lifelong goals, such as developing their own skills and those of the people they work with. This kind of self-motivation requires discipline, but it can be quite rewarding.

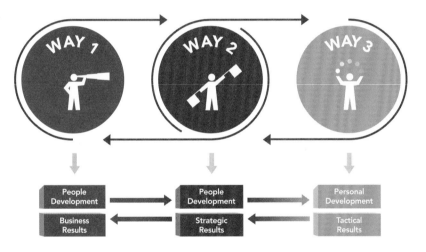

Way Three thinkers need to have specialized knowledge or skills while maintaining a broad perspective. Big companies in particular need employees who can learn specialties quickly. No one should assume that the expertise they have today will suffice tomorrow, so a willingness to learn is critical. Being a SME is critical. But being able to become a SME as technologies and models evolve is just as critical.

The ideal Way Three is someone we call when a task has to be done on time, on budget, and without mistakes. They have a sense of curiosity, desire, and a drive to work tirelessly at a task and assume extra duties.

Take another look at the flow, or arrows, of communication. While the Way Ones provide the ideas, they don't always do it alone. Idea is not just a four-letter word—it is how ideas are expressed, communicated, and brought to action that is relevant. A Way One should have a regular roundtable with Way Twos and Threes for potential innovative breakthroughs. Sometimes it's OK to come to the table with many ideas, if you know that's the objective. You're not there to leave with a plan. You're there to sound out and build on ideas. Ideation can only come from people.

> No one should assume that the expertise they have today will suffice tomorrow, so a willingness to learn is critical.

From where they sit, each Way has a different vision and focus. The Way One has a 360-degree vision. The Way Two can see 180 degrees—straight ahead and left and right. The Way Threes focus only on what's straight ahead but does so with the most detail. This serves many purposes besides fleshing out ideas. This is not to say that Way Twos are narrow-minded and Way Threes have tunnel vision. Rather, it is a simple way of visualizing the type of focus that each Way must utilize for the success of the business. At the minimum it also helps identify the mind-set of Way Twos and Way Threes, showing who is thinking like a Way Two and who is thinking like a Way Three.

Sometimes the next rising Way Two shows himself. And sometimes the Way One realizes there's a whole component of an idea to which she's been blind. It's like the old story about the twelve-foot truck stuck under the eleven and a half–foot bridge. Some are arguing the bridge strut has to be cut away. Some argue the truck needs to be cut in half. Both sides are arguing over the cost and work it will take. And then along comes a disinterested kid who says, "Why not just let the air out of the tires?"

Sometimes a Way One will (or should) want to meet with Way Twos and Threes to "bounce an idea" off them. As mentioned before, the Way One is looking for a plan to go with his idea. He is looking for a qualified Way Two to understand the idea and create a plan to execute the idea, not for the Way Two to run out and start executing right away. This is the theory behind town hall meetings. When a high-ranking public official wants to hear from the people, she will have a town hall meeting to discuss the ideas and the plans that are the most impactful with her constituents. "Where the rubber meets the road," as they say.

The Way One wants to go directly to the tactics and get instant feedback and circumvent the Way Two lines of communication. This is similar to the CEO who schedules quarterly employee breakfast meetings. This is his opportunity to get instant feedback. You never know where the next big idea will come from or how this feedback will inspire a new solution to an existing challenge. Action in search of a plan is a waste of money and plan development without a well-thought-out set of actions is a waste of time. Therefore the Way Two and Three team is essential to determining if a plan is implementable or not by combining their thought processes and focusing on one issue.

A Way Three, a SME, can tell the Way Two if it will work. The problem exists when a disengaged or unqualified Way Three thinker is asked for input. As a result, the Way Two does not get the input required to validate the implementation of the plan. They are forced to do the investigation themselves (or proceed with poor or incomplete information), usually dealing in areas with which they are not familiar, and the plan ultimately gets kicked off and the plane gets built in flight. Balancing out the planning team with strategic and tactical thinkers is critical to the success of the plan. The success of the original idea (or a variation of the original idea), and ultimately the business result that the idea is connected to, is determined by the balanced thinkers and teamwork of the people involved. This also creates buy-in from the Way Twos and Way Threes because they have a hand in shaping the overall business objective. ROE is the game we play at work. ROE is teamwork.

SECTION VII

Apply ROE Now

eleven

Organizational Development

*Even if you are on the right track, you will
get run over if you just sit there.*
—Will Rogers

We've seen how to apply the ROE methodology to our dealings with others, regardless of which seat they occupy or which Way they think. We've seen how it can be used to increase ROE (and thus ROI) whether dealing within an organization or approaching one from the outside. We've seen it used in leadership, management, sales, and marketing.

But what about an organization's most important resources: organizational effectiveness and viability? In this chapter, we're going to talk about organizational development and specifically how it relates to process and self-analysis. We call this the ROE Gap. We'll talk about how to hire the right kind of people based on what their Way is, and we'll also talk about how to get hired or promoted depending on what Way you are.

As noted earlier, it's the supreme historical folly of American businesses that employees (as measured by payroll costs) are listed on the liability side of the balance sheet instead of assets. How much of that mind-set derives from broken arrows, the inability to see the limitations and strengths of each Way of thinking and the necessity of fulfilling the seats of the Way Ones, Way Twos, and Way Threes? Process is without question essential to the organization.

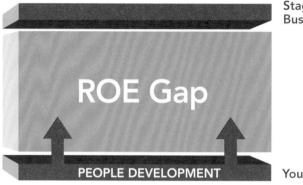

Stage in the
Business Life Cycle

Your Skill Level

A complete understanding and implementation of the ROE methodology has a critical role in organizational development—both for the employer and the employment seeker and how they fit over time as the business evolves. ROE helps organizations conduct better interviews, which in turn leads to a stronger team of employees. Additionally, the methodology can serve as a guide to job seekers in interviews and in earning promotions within an organization. But ROE must also be used at people and organization evaluation periods as well. Otherwise you will not be able to close the ROE Gap. The ROE Gap is the difference in the current skill level of the Way and how that Way should be thinking and communicating based upon what stage the organization is in on the corporate life cycle (see figure on page 99). The bar to determine the ROE Gap is the difference between these two points.

> Even if you are on the right track, you will get left behind if you don't constantly improve your skills.

The quote at the beginning of this chapter is, "Even if you are on the right track, you will get run over if you just sit there." I love this quote, but might suggest that it read, "Even if you are on the right track, you will get left behind if you don't constantly improve your skills," because as soon as the organization progresses to the next stage in the corporate life cycle, if your skills don't progress with it, the ROE Gap gets wider and you might get left behind or need to be replaced with someone who can close the Gap. A victim of the ROE Gap is more commonly referred to as someone "in over their head" or "trying to keep their head above water." The water line is where the company is on the business life cycle; your head is your skill level.

I spoke earlier of a business college graduate who was being interviewed by an organization's Way One for a Way Two position—a position for which she was not qualified in terms of experience. However, the Way One consistently described the job in terms of a series of Way Three seat tasks. After asking her a series of questions, we both realized the Way One had no real plan, only ideas and a Way Two job description that involved many Way Three tasks. He had no real vision for what he wanted the Way Two position to be. He only had a list of Way Three tasks, which he wanted carried out by someone who could fill the role. The interview and subsequent offer never involved the strategic thinking a Way Two is ultimately responsible for delivering— which was the position for which she was interviewing. Again, people walk around all the time with the wrong title.

As I said before, my first thought was that if she was going to be hired to be both a Way Two and a Way Three, she should get two paychecks. In smaller businesses people must wear many hats and sit in more than one seat; that's not the point. The reason I said two paychecks is because the Way One did not understand that she would be performing two jobs—two different Ways of thinking from two different seats. The skill

> The two results that should be connected to the Way One are people development and business results, in that order.

level he seemed to want was aligned to a Way Three position, but she was interviewing for a Way Two position. We realized that ultimately she was inadvertently being set up for failure. She could easily perform all the Way Three tasks, but because she had no avenue to contribute the kind of strategic performance and results that a Way One expects of a Way Two, she would be seen as underperforming. She passed on the offer because there were other opportunities and it was going to take too much to try to communicate to the Way One how underprepared he really was.

Of course, human resources isn't just about hiring or being hired; it's about the integration of your human resources into the process and developing their skill sets in order to stay ahead of the pace of the organization. This is something that is close to the heart of every Way One. After all, the two results that should be connected to the Way One are people development and business results, in that order.

For instance, a client hires managers who play a very strategic role in the company. They hire very good managers. But they are often MBA graduates who have never sat in a Way Three seat. The company will take that newly hired Way Two manager and send them to work with the affiliated advertising agency to learn how their jobs fit into the bigger picture.

This isn't initially cost-effective. It's poor ROI and poor ROE. Instead of spending tens of thousands to send these new managers thousands of miles away to work as virtual interns, they should first consider sending them to the Way Three seat to see how their plans are going to be implemented. This will give them a better idea of how the Way Threes work and what the Way Threes need in terms of turning abstract campaigns into implementable tasks. They can also assess the skill level of their new team to see which Way they think, which will determine the most efficient way to utilize their skill sets in their plans. They can see how the Way Threes interact with the public, clients, and vendors so that they get a better idea of where the rubber meets the road in terms of the deliverables involved in campaigns.

One of our clients is a major national nonprofit, and we often work with one of their Way Twos. She was having trouble dealing with unmotivated Way Threes, but she didn't know where the arrow was breaking down or if the Way Threes were not getting what they needed. In turn, this inevitably affected how she met the needs of the Way One. Her skills as a Way Two for marketing were second to none. Her own skills and management for her piece of the pie were not the problem. The problem was that she did not know how to properly mentor and motivate the Way Threes. Once we helped her mentor and motivate, she saw her own need for development and what she needed to develop in others. Managing and mentoring are as different as managing and leading.

Someone being interviewed for a job or promotion ends up dealing with a variety of people, and that changes depending on the different stages of a company—from start-up to small business to larger corporation. Someone interviewing at a small company might end up speaking to the owner, to the vice president of sales, and to the administrative assistant. At a larger company you're likely dealing with an outside headhunter agency, dedicated human resources department, the department head for the division in question, and often a Way Three who may be acting as a team leader.

Regardless of the setup, almost invariably the interviewers will have been dealing with a large number of applicants. If I'm the person being interviewed, my natural question for myself is, "How do I stand out?"

There are the usual how-to books for professional interviewing and they are useful. Consider them the minimum that you want to bring to the table. But the minimum is not what gets noticed. This is where the application of the ROE methodology serves the individual as much as it serves an organization.

If I'm that applicant, as soon as I know to whom I'm speaking I can tailor my conversation. You're not changing your message or telling interviewers what they want to hear; you're speaking to them on a level and in the language that is most accessible to them. You are connecting them to their desired results.

Invariably, interviews go both ways. The applicant is asked a number of open-ended questions that are really prompts to an open dialogue. The applicant is also asked to pose their own questions about the position, the company, and the industry.

A Way One will often end up trying to sell a prospective employee on the company, and the prospective employee won't get a chance to sell themselves. If I'm interviewing for a Way Three role, I might be either overwhelmed or inspired by their passion and enthusiasm.

If I'm speaking with the Way One about a Way Three position, I'm not going to spend a lot of time talking about details of the tasks I'm expected to perform, or how smart I am with the tools I'm expected to use—at least not at the start. I want to first connect him with his results. I might ask what the vision for the company is and how my job impacts that vision. I would ask, "What five business objectives have been set for the year? How can I help you get there?" I would appeal to their passion and vision and link the position for which I am interviewing directly to their own expectations.

If it's a Way Two with whom I'm speaking, then I go into some specifics:

- Who would I report to?
- Is your strategy solid?
- Are you on plan?
- If not, how can I help?
- Where do you see me fitting into the plan?
- What gaps can I fill to ensure we are on plan?
- Are your ideas being implemented?
- How many times has the one-year strategic plan changed over the past year?

By asking these questions, I'm interviewing the interviewer, but I'm also addressing the very reasons they need this position filled. How do I know if my future boss is a micromanager or one with the skill set to manage people and not jump in and *do* the work? With the talent pool as deep as it is right now, they know they can hire someone who can impact ROE immediately. And speaking to them in this fashion shows that you are that person. You're not someone who is good at doing interviews but really just wants to punch a clock and get a paycheck. You are someone who will start with—and maintain—strong arrows of communication.

A Way Three should further ask a Way Two interviewer, "What's the forum in which we can share ideas in order to get ownership or plan verification?" Maybe this particular Way Two has never had the luxury of working with qualified Way Threes and this would be a new experience for them. Ask, "What are your five main business objectives? Are you happy with the plan? Happy with what is being done to support the brand? What SME experience can I bring to the plan that would help you?"

Then you can really be in sync with the Way Two when you ask, "How can I knock this three-step process down to two? Do you have a strong arrow with the Way One so that we can bring ideas to action without negatively affecting the Way Two's existing plan?"

> ROE helps you keep your boss's boss off your boss's back.

Again, you'll be speaking to the interviewer about their pain—about the results to which they are held accountable—and it will certainly differentiate you from other candidates. Furthermore, you can determine if you have a Way Three thinker in a Way Two seat who would be your future mentor. At this point, you know what the consequences of this mismatch can be. ROE helps you keep your boss's boss off your boss's back.

I once had a seminar participant, Jim, tell me, "I'm not a Way Three; I'm a Way Four." Of course he was joking, but what he meant was that he was a Way Three who didn't know how to advance to the next level. He was stuck at the bottom of the traditional organizational chart. Jim had tried to sell himself to the Way One, telling the Way One what a great job he'd been doing. But what Jim didn't see was that from the Way One's way of seeing things, it's not about Jim. It's about the company's results and understanding why Jim was doing what he was doing.

The Way One wants to see that Jim is tied to the business objectives—and ultimately, results—through the implementation of his tactics. Jim needed to show the Way One that he was developing himself so that he could have more direct impact on the company's results and the Way One's vision. Furthermore, he needed to explain that his tasks were positively impacting the plan that was directly tied to his business objectives. That's effective communication.

We once discovered that an employee of mine was spending her off time taking a software course that would increase her efficiency and proficiency. That showed she had a passion to build on her skill level, and that is characteristic of a budding Way Two who needs mentoring so she can fulfill her potential for herself and for the company growth.

In job interviews and promotions, people tend to be more interested in virtues and characteristics and less in their specific skills that are aligned with the tasks that will ultimately determine if they are a success at the position. They talk about their positive characteristics and they are showcasing their best social behavior. On the other side of the table, employers want to identify the virtues they need in the person they are hiring. Of course, they don't ask, "Are you trustworthy?" That's what references are for. But what often ends up happening is that someone is hired based more on personality than skills. We've all heard stories of people hired because they interviewed so well, but they didn't bring any skills beyond being a good interviewee.

I want to interview someone for his or her skills. I want to know if they are SMEs and if they are quick learners. They don't have to be perfect in their skills. I let them know that we're going to help develop their tools and skills and hone them. I want to know, though, if they have the fundamental skills upon which to build. Are you truly an expert at Excel spreadsheets, or do you just know how to use it? If you are a Way Two, how would you manage a Way Three to stay on plan? Do you know how to first assess the skill and characteristics of an unmotivated Way Three and then mentor and motivate? How have you communicated respectfully and reliably to a Way One before? Are you a bridge builder—do you strengthen or weaken arrows? Are you a brainstormer and good at idea-bouncing? How have you done that before, and how did it impact the strategic plan?

With the tools of the ROE methodology, I can quickly identify if someone is truly a Way Three or Way Two thinker, regardless of the title on their business card. People walk around with the wrong title all the time. Are they speaking a lot about managing tasks, or managing a plan? If I communicate with them about planning and strategy and they engage in that conversation, I can tell if they are a qualified Way Two or if they are a Way Three aspiring to become a Way Two, but who would end up diving into the weeds and micromanaging. If the candidate is the latter, I know I can use them as a Way Three while mentoring them to become a fully qualified Way Two.

Organization development is the attempt to influence the members of an organization to expand their candidness with each other about their views of the organization and their experience in it, and to encourage them to take greater responsibility for their own actions as organization members. The assumption behind OD is that when people pursue both of these objectives simultaneously, they are likely to discover new ways of working together that are more effective for achieving their own and their shared organizational goals. When this does not happen, such activity helps them understand why it has not and aids in making meaningful choices about what to do in light of this understanding.

I had a client recently ask, "Why would I knowingly put a Way Two thinker in a Way Three seat?" I told the client that the unemployment rate is so high right now that some people are willing to take on any work for a paycheck. If someone is overqualified for their job, do you think they will be happy and stay long-term? Probably not unless the organization is changing so rapidly that the rate of organizational growth catches up with their thinking and the seat they occupy. In this case they have a negative ROE Gap. Placing a Way Two thinker in a Way Three seat could have great benefits in the short term. Maybe there is a bold new initiative being developed. Having a well-balanced team with a group of qualified thinkers could be an insurance policy to help make it successful. I told my client that if it is important to have someone who can see the bigger picture, and if he can be managed as such, then it might be a good fit.

But if the position you desire to fill is one in which he will perform a task and go home, and the company is not on an aggressive growth path, then it probably is not a good fit. They ended up placing the hire, but used him in a more strategic role while also having him perform the intended tasks. This is the role consultants sometimes play: a super-qualified SME who can swoop in, do the work of a team of people in a nonpermanent position, and set up the desired strategy with an execution schedule all tied to a business result.

If you are that Way Three looking to become a Way Two or a Way One, there are other ways in which you can help yourself that don't involve being mentored. We've mentioned before that sometimes a person who sits in a Way Two seat at work might be a Way One thinker on her church's fundraising committee. The Way Three in financing might develop his skills as a Way One as the coach of the company softball team. Whether it's volunteering to lead a scout troop or helping to direct an industry-associated philanthropy committee, you develop those skills by exercising those muscles. Sitting in that seat of responsibility broadens your perspective, which at the very least will help you strengthen your arrow to your own Way Two or Way One because you can better understand their perspective. After all, the best way to learn something is by teaching it to someone else.

Too much time in business is spent trying to fit square pegs into round holes and expecting lemon trees to produce oranges. By strengthening the arrows from the start of the hiring and promotion process and by using the ROE methodology to cut through the static and pleasantries, we can fit round pegs to round holes and set the company and its employees up for success.

Unfortunately the right hire today might not be the right hire for tomorrow. It is difficult to forecast change. A qualified Way One with a clear vision may be able to see the change that might need to occur in the future to keep developing his organization. Maybe the 180-degree vision is enough to accurately predict the anticipated changes. We manage business differently in the start-up phase compared to the infancy, adolescent, and adulthood phases.

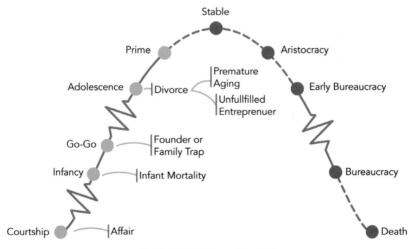

Dr. Ichak Adizes Model

"Every organization grows and develops according to a natural life cycle, facing predictable problems at each stage along the way."

—Dr. Ichak Adizes

Companies usually start out top-heavy, or heavy on the left side as in the ROE communication chain. As the company grows, are the skill sets and proper Ways of thinking growing with it? Why is it that the founder is rarely the Way One when the company enters a later, more developed and profitable stage in the corporate life cycle? And there is only one Way One. What about the migration of the business along the corporate life cycle and all the Way Twos and Threes along the way? Do they have the adulthood skills at the infancy stage? What is being done to plan for that? Does this new hire have the ability to grow with the company? What people development initiatives are the company going to partake in to ensure that the right thinkers with the right characteristics are developed into the next Way of thinking? Are the Ways growing at the same rate as the company?

I know I should be on the bus. I am sitting in the right seat—now, how am I thinking and communicating?

People development—ROE—is the key to ensuring that the people who are around during these stage transitions are the right thinkers in the right seats. We, with good reason, focus on the company's products, services, competition, marketing, sales, branding, and rebranding, but what about the core development of the people and organization? Even if a well-funded start-up company had the benefit of overhiring for each position, this would still be a challenge. If the right qualified thinker is not in the right seat at the right time, then all the money in the world might not move the needle. A mediocre plan implemented well far exceeds a great plan implemented poorly.

Big start-up money is great, but keeping the powder dry and focusing on the balance of the human resource pool is what's ultimately best for the stockholders, the company, the employees, and its customers. If, in theory, an ROE manager was hired to assess the types of thinkers aligned to the seat they currently occupy and the seat that will need to be occupied once growth takes effect, then the employees can be moved in, out, or around the organizational chart to have the biggest impact on results.

Sun Tzu is overquoted in the business world, owing to too many executives thinking it makes them sound more macho. But one saying rarely mentioned is—and I paraphrase—"If you know yourself and you know your opponent, you need not fear the outcome of a thousand battles." Taking the core of this to the twenty-first-century world of enterprise, from the company's perspective, it means that if you know what function you need fulfilled and if you truly know the Way in which a candidate thinks, the outcome of that hire or promotion is entirely predictable, and you won't be disappointed. If you're the job seeker and you know your own virtues, characteristics, and skills, and you truly understand what it is the company needs from their hire, you can know whether you're being set up for success or inadvertently set up for failure.

In all cases, it comes down to knowing the Way people are thinking, where they are sitting at what stage in the development of the organization, and where they want to sit. Are their personal and professional goals aligned? ROE is entirely applicable to your personal life as well—maybe that should be my next book.

It's worth considering that, as the Ways of thinking fall under vision, strategy, and tactics, an organization could fall within the same type of thinking. Is Apple a Way One company that is visionary? Is GM a Way Three company that's about the tactics? Could they reinvent themselves and become a Way One company that thinks innovatively with an outside-the-box attitude?

twelve

ROE Marketing

*The only thing that's worse than being blind
is having sight but no vision.*
—Helen Keller

Marketing is the process of teaching consumers why they should choose your product or service over that of your competitors; if you are not doing that, you are not marketing. It's really that simple. The key is finding the right method and defining the right message to use to educate and influence your consumers.

Marketing is everything that you do to reach and persuade prospects. The sales process is everything that you do to close the sale and get a signed agreement or contract. The difference between the two is creating demand versus converting demand. Both are necessities for the success of a business. You cannot do without either process. You have to ensure strong communication between qualified thinkers of marketing and sales to strategically combine both efforts in a way that ensures sales success and is tied to business objectives. Strong arrows of communication, which lead to a strong Return on Energy, are critical here.

Too many companies don't tie their marketing strategy to tactics. All the glorious and creative campaigns, complete with bells, whistles, and music that makes your heart swell, won't mean a thing if the frontline people don't believe in it, or if no one understands it. All of the money tied up in your marketing campaign—in advertising, PR, logos, brands—all of that is wasted if you don't have ownership from the people at the front door. You may have done all your homework and articulated your brand and mission in a great campaign, but when the customer arrives and is greeted by a surly receptionist, a lackadaisical baggage handler, or an Apple salesperson who talks over your head and makes you uncomfortable, then you might have just as well set that money on fire.

Of course, long before you work on creating, executing, and maximizing ROE on a marketing strategy, you have to have maximized ROE within your company. If your Way One is mired in details and your Way Two is micromanaging the Way Threes and the Way Threes run out the clock on the day, all the marketing in the world won't help. It's like putting high-octane fuel in a car that's up on blocks. You have to fix the equation—the engine— using ROE.

Is the Way One communicating to the Way Two a sense of why customers buy from their company? Is the Way Two communicating to the Way Three what the Way Three could offer that would attract more customers? Is the Way Three communicating the information about the competition she gains while on a sales call to the Way Two so that the Way Two and Way One might get a better sense of overall market trends? Is the Way Two communicating to the Way Three sufficiently to ensure that the Way Three can explain to the client the advantages of their product over the competition's?

Is the Way Two who is in charge of distribution and delivery sufficiently managing Way Three delivery people so that they understand how critical deadlines and delivery ETAs are? Are sales people learning about how the company's brand and position is perceived and reporting it back to the Way Two in a manner that allows the Way Two to ensure it is on the right track?

Ensuring strong arrows from Way One to Two, and Two to Three, is critical to maximizing your marketing ROE.

Great companies that consistently have success are companies with great brands. Think of companies who cast a shadow even bigger than the actual percentage of the market for which they account. Nike, Coca-Cola, Apple, and Starbucks, for instance, are so universally known that it doesn't matter where you live—you know what they are.

Long before the iPhone and iPad became consumer must-haves, Apple was the talk of the computer world. As recently as the early 1990s, the argument from PC users against buying a Mac was that Apple only had about 10 percent of market share for personal computers, and therefore there wasn't much in the way of software or games available for Mac users. And yet, the thing to note is that people were talking about Mac even then. Apple's brand was already blazing. People were drawn to its intuitive functionality and stylish design, even though almost every system out there supported Windows and Bill Gates was doing his best to lock down the whole of the software and hardware world.

By the time Apple launched the iPhone in the early 2000s, people were buzzing about what a game-changer the device was even though they'd never seen a true smart phone in action. Apple had built such confidence in its brand that when they said the iPhone was a new kind of communication, people believed it.

> Great brands aren't built in the marketing department.

Great brands aren't built in the marketing department. The deliverables that support the brand are. The slogans that reflect the brand and the icons that identify it are. But brands are built in every division of a company. Clients and customers might be impressed with your catchy logo and your mission statement, but if that's the only place your brand lives then it's not a successful brand. A successful brand is built when every employee of the company understands the vision of the company and how their role—their tasks or their strategic management—contributes to the achievement and realization of that vision.

Apple's brand is stylish, smart, user-friendly, and casual. It's reflected in the design of their software. It's in the sleekness of iPads, iPhones, and MacBook Airs. It's ensured by the quality assurance performed for every third-party app. But it goes much further than that. At the Apple stores, Apple employees are exceptionally well-educated on every product. They can walk even a novice through their most complex software. They dress stylishly and casually. They are user-friendly in the same way that the software is. The same is true for customer service at the Genius Bar, where their technicians walk you through repairs and upgrades in the same informal, easy-to-follow manner. They even offer free classes on various software suites.

Everything done by Apple from concept to sale stays true to the Apple brand.

There is one company, though, that is the exemplar of owning a brand that permeates every level of the company and has the ownership and support of everyone from the entry-level trainees to the CEO. That company is Southwest Airlines.

Southwest Airlines is regularly named in CEO surveys as the No. 1 brand in American business, as reported by the American City Business Journals. Asked to describe its success, Godfrey Phillips, vice president for research at ACBJ, said the airline ranks No. 1 for several reasons: "One, it's a value brand, which is critical; two, it was built by an entrepreneur and has an entrepreneurial attitude; and three, they don't nickel-and-dime you—and [small and midsize business owners] hate to be nickel-and-dimed."

Southwest Airlines is built on the idea that loyalty begins with the employees. In fact, their ability to be profitable depends entirely on them. Flying short-distance flights is, according to conventional wisdom, an unprofitable approach as planes are forced to spend a greater portion of time on the ground than in the air. But rather than cutting labor costs and buying cheap equipment, Southwest relies on their employees to create profit by putting more planes in the air through quick turnarounds.

Strong internal relationships ensure that proper information is passed between individuals when they need it. Employees are hired for their perfect fit into the Southwest culture as much as they are for any job-related qualifications. When something goes wrong, unlike most airlines, there's no quest to blame an individual or department. Instead, a much more positive work environment is created in which everyone works together to find out what went wrong and how it can be prevented in the future.

Most airlines favor a method where one individual is in control of many flights via a computer system. For Southwest, the focus remains on person-to-person interaction. Agents are assigned to only one flight at a time and interact directly with other people in the operation, rather than through a computer or telephone. Not only does this face-to-face interaction facilitate relationship building, it also helps minimize time deficits produced by unforeseen circumstances that would otherwise result in untimely delays caused by lack of communication.

This strong focus and dependence on employee relations ensures that everyone who is working for Southwest really wants to work at Southwest. There's no hierarchy between pilots and baggage handlers. Everyone is working together to better serve the customer and they're happy to do it. Not only does their state of mind create a positive atmosphere for the customers, but their efficient, communication-focused approach has resulted in fewer lost bags, fewer delays, and inevitably, fewer complaints.

As proven by Southwest, the hardest thing for marketing to do is to try to go it alone. When marketing creates a brand or message that is not necessarily embraced in other departments, it's going nowhere. Marketing is highly conceptual. People who end up in other departments are there because they aren't conceptual—they are more task-oriented and left-brained. ROE is

> Marketing is everything that the consumer encounters when it comes to your business.

a practical methodology for conveying important, highly conceptual ideas in a way that allows the ideas to be embraced and practiced.

Companies make the mistake of thinking that marketing is just "one" thing, but marketing is everything that the consumer encounters when it comes to your business, from advertising, to what they hear, to the customer service that they receive, to the follow-up care that you provide. It's all marketing and it all creates the decision by the consumer of whether or not to choose you initially or for repeat business.

The activities of marketing are often confused with advertising and sales, but it is important to realize that there is a difference. You need to see marketing as the wide range of activities involved in making sure that you're continuing to meet the needs of your customers and are getting value in return. Marketing analysis includes finding out what groups of potential customers (or markets) exist, what groups of customers you prefer to serve (target markets), what their needs are, what products or services you might develop to meet their needs, how the customers might prefer to use the products and services, what your competitors are doing, what pricing you should use, and how you should distribute products and services to your target markets. Various methods of market research are used to find out information about markets, target markets, and their needs, competitors, etc. Marketing also includes ongoing promotions, which can include advertising, public relations, sales, and customer service.

Advertising is a single component of the marketing process. It's the part that involves getting the word out concerning your business, product, or the services you are offering. It involves the process of developing strategies such as ad placement, frequency, and so on. Advertising includes the placement of an ad in such mediums as newspapers, direct mail, billboards, television, radio, and of course, the Internet. Advertising is the largest expense of most marketing plans, with public relations following in a close second, and market research not falling far behind.

Think of marketing as a pie. Inside that pie you have slices of advertising, market research, media planning, public relations, product pricing, distribution, customer support, sales strategy, and community involvement. Advertising only equals one piece of the pie in the strategy. All of these elements must not only work independently but also work together toward the bigger goal. Marketing is a process that takes time and can involve hours of research for a marketing plan to be effective. Think of marketing as everything that an organization does to facilitate an exchange between company and consumer.

A client for an international executive protection firm and former Navy SEAL once asked me, "This methodology is so simple; why is business so hard?" It's because simple doesn't mean easy. "Eat fewer calories than you burn" is the simple way to lose weight. But as anyone who has dieted before can tell you, that doesn't make it easy.

ROE and maintaining strong arrows among employees are critical strategies in creating a brand that succeeds and a company that works.

thirteen

ROE Trusted Advisor

Pretend everyone is wearing a sign that says,
"I want to feel special."
—Jack Rose

As we've seen, people in different positions within an organization see through a prism that is colored by their role. This is true whether it's a multinational corporation or a small café. If you're at that café and you have a good experience, the waiter—if he is a motivated Way Three and therefore interested in consistently improving the service he renders—will want to know the details that made your experience such a positive one. He will ask you detailed questions about the service, if the wine pairings he suggested worked, and if his advice about the dessert was helpful.

Let's say it's the manager, though, who asks you how your meal was, and you mention it was a great experience. As a Way Two, she will care more about the Way Three performance than about the immediate details of the whole experience. Was the ambiance what you desired? Was the meal what you'd hoped for? Did you enjoy having live music from the piano player? Will you tell your friends?

The owner, meanwhile, will want to know how her restaurant compared to your other favorite eateries. Did you enjoy the subtle difference that a Baja-inspired menu makes, given that most

Mexican restaurant menus are informed by the Yucatan style of cooking? Did the meal enhance the experience, the birthday, reception, etc.? Will the memory be tied to the restaurant?

Again and again, you'll see that determining the best way to communicate with someone all comes down to which Way that person is thinking and the seat with which that thinking is aligned. The person who is poised to benefit most from this is the one who has cultivated a global awareness of the three Ways and who can change focus as needed without losing the core message.

In sales this can make the difference between success and failure. For starters, no matter whom you are selling to—the Way One, Two, or Three—and regardless of what you are selling, you are not selling a product; you are providing a solution, a result. To provide a solution you need to know what the real problem, the source of the pain, is. As the saying goes, you need to ask yourself if you're selling the drills or the holes. You're selling the value— the end result—not the tool. You're selling an improved Return on Energy within the organization, and what's important is that you explain this in a tailored manner to whatever Way is making the decision. If you cannot obtain the necessary information to come up with a prescription for the pain, you may first need to perform an arrow analysis in order to deliver results.

When you're selling to a Way One, you talk about bottom-line business results and increasing employee efficiency. The qualified Way One doesn't care whether it turns clockwise or counterclockwise, if it uses Microsoft or Apple software, or if you make all deliveries before ten in the morning. Of course, those questions might come up, but first things first. Way One thinking starts at the macro level. There is simply not enough time in the day to process all the details. As we say, Way Ones have more money than time. Way Ones must feel comfortable with making decisions with good information, good facts. They want to be presented with good quality information at a high level. So communicate with them as their trusted advisors do, as their Way Two.

If they cannot make an educated decision with what is presented, they will dive deeper into the strategy or deeper yet into the tactics, but it has to be their calling. If a CEO starts with the tactics, you might be dealing with a Way Three thinker in a Way One seat, which is an opportunity if he possesses the right characteristics for people development. Mentoring into Way One thinking will establish you as an incredible value-add beyond your product or service. Be ready if he switches to Way One thinking and know how to tie the details of what you are selling to people development or business results. A qualified Way One thinker will make decisions under those principles.

I've always asked Way Ones to breakfast or early morning coffee, respecting their time. Even if I run into the Way One in the elevator, I'm always prepared with a people development or business results elevator pitch, not about my company per se, but something like, "Mr. CEO, it was exciting to see sales increase by 5 percent last quarter with the dimensional mailer we created and used in the holiday direct marketing campaign." Or, "It is great working with Mrs. Marketing Manager. The marketing strategy she developed to impact the increasing gross margin business objective is dead-on. I am developing new product ideas that will compliment the plan perfectly."

Sometimes—even better—if you are already seen as a value driver, it could be a great opportunity to get answers to questions that your contacts have not been able to answer, especially if you are dealing with a broken arrow from him to your Way Two contact. Maybe it is information that could allow you to deliver a more appropriate product than what was originally asked of you, and this is a great opportunity to make your contact look good!

In order for the organization to develop, the people within it must stay ahead of the development curve and close the ROE Gap, which means that the company not only meets goals, but also continues to create new goals as they go along. If they don't develop, the resistance will create a pull on the organization, keeping it from advancing to the next stage of growth and profitability, instead of the people within it pushing the organization along. People development (i.e., leadership and mentoring, managing and mentoring, and self-improvement in all the Ways) and an awareness of ROE will definitely help create this push effect.

Outside resources such as vendors, suppliers, salespeople, and others help play a critical role in the push effect, too. Rarely is this option considered as a value-add in the product and service delivery space. But of course the supplier's organization should also employ ROE in this organization–organization relationship in order for the push effect to benefit all.

The Way Two buyer has his own way of looking at buying what you're selling. They want to know if this product will complement their strategic plan and if it can be integrated into the implementation quickly and easily. They want to know if it will streamline processes and speed up production. They want to know if it will improve the output of their Way Threes so that they can report to the Way One with those words every Way One wants to hear: "We are on plan." Or even better, "We're on plan and ahead of schedule." (If you can add "and under budget," that's pretty much the perfect hat trick.)

Sometimes the person of influence on a sale is the Way Three. That's where you get into the details—how it works and what it does. The Way Three wants to know if the software is customizable. He wants to know where the buttons are, where the cloud is, how fast it runs, how much it can be upgraded, and what add-on applications are in the pipeline. He wants to know how this software will take his ten tasks and knock it down to five. He wants to look good to the Way he reports to. The information you provide may not be completely understood, but if presented in the right way, it will serve to develop their skills (positioning you as a value-add) and be available as valuable information for the decision maker.

That Way Three is sitting across the table from you and he's asking one unspoken question: "How will this make *my* life and work easier?"

You need to have that answer ready. You need to know the details of what you're selling. You need to know how it will answer their *what* questions.

I worked with an account executive who tried to convert a Way Three prospect for over a year. She tried everything. This was a hard sell because the prospect was an unmotivated Way Three thinker. The information we received was very tactical in nature with no ties to strategy whatsoever. Identifying it was a big challenge. Therefore a lot of ROE on our side had to be invested to establish a strong arrow from her Way Two boss to her in order to even begin suggesting a solution that would work.

Then one day, the account executive simply said, "Lori, I am here to make you look good." With that we went to work repairing the broken arrow from the Way Two to the Way Three and back again—not selling our product. We started asking Lori strategy-type questions. She then had to go to her boss to get the answers. We were in effect developing her thought process into that of a highly motivated Way Three thinker so she could understand why she was doing what she was doing—in other words, understanding the strategy to which her tasks were tied.

When we received the information we needed, two things happened: One, Lori's boss began to feel that Lori had a clearer understanding of her job and started to include her in more of the planning process, which in turn established buy-in and gave her ownership. Two, we got the information we needed to accomplish the strategic results that our tactics and our products were designed to accomplish. Needless to say, Lori was somewhat underappreciated in the company and was not very involved, not because she couldn't do the job but because no one—including Lori—had developed her.

By using ROE, Lori was able to position herself in the company as a valuable resource in plan development and we were able to deliver on our promise and make her look good by positioning ourselves as a valuable vendor resource. When the campaign was over, her boss's sales team sent her flowers for her involvement in the project. This could have gone completely differently if we simply would have delivered to her what she originally requested— what vendors had been delivering for years. We, however, used ROE to focus on people development first and business results second—ROE over ROI.

Way Threes want to look good for their Way Two. They need their questions answered and for the deliverable to increase their ROE. But sometimes the arrow between the Way Three and the Way Two is broken, as was the case with Lori and the Way to whom she reports.

As you are there to sell a result, not a widget, you can see the opportunities this creates for you in terms of providing solutions and connecting people to their desired result.

You can help strengthen the arrow from the Way Three to the Way Two. This provides a benefit for the buyer and the company as a whole. It creates a sense of partnership, not just a simple vendor relationship. When I'm asked how we deliver value in a commoditized business I say, "We strengthen arrows and connect

Ways to the right results." When a trusted advisor can strengthen or repair a broken arrow, that's value! For instance, let's say the Way Three isn't sure if your product will work for their needs and budget. The Way Three needs to get more information to make the right decision or influence the one who needs to make the right decision.

You can arm the Way Three with the right questions they can ask their Way Two. Sometimes they just need to know the right questions to show the Way Two the breadth of their own thinking and vision. It helps support the Way Three's efforts to think beyond his tasks and think more about how his role fits into the strategy and how that supports that company's vision and business objectives. By bringing these smart questions to the Way Two, the arrow from Three to Two is strengthened. The Way Two can then better explain why the product is needed—not just what is needed—and that leaves both you and the Way Three better equipped to deliver the right solution.

Don't underestimate the Way Three as your customer. Way

Threes are the gatekeepers. They are the target's outer circle with which you first come into contact. When you help secure that Way Three's seat at the table, that Way Three will secure your seat at the table as well. And if the gate is opened to her Way Two, start with solutions that connect the Way Two to their desired results and start asking questions about business objectives, always staying a step ahead. I know you know that at this point, it's less about the tactics when sitting at the Way Two table. Start evaluating the strength of the Way One to Way Two arrow.

> Practice ROE in the sales position, and delivering value and producing happy, profitable clients will be yours.

Pretty simple, huh? Remember, though, that simple does not mean easy. Practice ROE in the sales position, and delivering value and producing happy, profitable clients will be yours.

Sales is like marketing in the sense that with a marketing message, you only have a few seconds to grab someone's attention. You have a very limited time to get your message across effectively. The best way to accomplish this is to understand to whom you're speaking and what their desired results are. That's why you have to determine before you start just which Way the decision maker is for the kind of sale you are looking to make. Going in with the wrong approach is no different from bringing a football to a baseball game.

But don't be tricked by the ones who are, for example, Way Three thinkers in Way Two seats. Sure, explain away on the details, but help them see how your product or service can be tied to a strategy. This is the mentoring process, but the caveat is that you may not be getting paid for your time and sometimes it is not worth your ROE investment. The rule of thumb is that a difficult prospect may be a difficult client. If this is an uphill battle, maybe it is not worth your ROE to make your customer smarter unless you are getting paid for it or there is a big windfall down the line.

Imagine how the Way One feels managing a Way Three thinker in a Way Two seat.

If you start talking to a Way One about very detailed aspects of your widget, their eyes will glaze over and they will want you to go away. The Way One has more money than time. I always respect this law. They don't see or care about the value of optimizing their software or the widget maker with the crank on the left-hand side. You have to align your messages effectively with their Way of thinking. You have to think about the ROE for that person. That Way One will perk up when you speak to his passion about the business and how the adoption of your product will improve his ROE at all points along the communication chain, thus helping to realize and achieve the long-term vision for the company.

Keep in mind the vast differences between entrepreneur and enterprise organizations and the thinkers who are involved. Entrepreneurs, especially in start-up phases, are thinking like all the Ways each day, bouncing from one seat to the next. Enterprise CxOs are anchored to a more consistent way of thinking. Either way, the ROE sales strategy works. They don't call it entrepreneurial attention deficit disorder for nothing. When communicating with a Way One of a start-up venture or a well-established small business who chooses to stay small, the salesperson who knows how to quickly address all three Ways and the results connecting to each respectively will be the one who delivers value—not just a product or service. Sometimes this three-way conversation occurs with the same person. Under normal circumstances, this could be incredibly confusing, but with ROE as your guide, it becomes very manageable and worthwhile.

As innovative as the ROE methodology is, it is not some untested academic theory. It works in practice every time.

> A sales meeting is as much about intelligence gathering as it is about selling.

It's been honed and fine-tuned in the proving ground of real-world sales experience.

A sales meeting is as much about intelligence gathering as it is about selling. You are there to provide solutions and value and to do this you must ask smart questions and get smart answers from qualified sources. These smart questions, and ultimately smart answers, will accomplish business objectives. They will help to determine which of the many strategies devised by a company are useful. Once you identify where the pain is—or which arrow needs repairing—the type of thinkers in each seat, and the desired results that need to be accomplished, your solutions and your true value to the organization is not far away. In other words, your effort to deliver value or, as they say, solution selling is actually increasing your prospect's or client's Return on Energy. If you're just there selling a product or service, something is deeply flawed. You cannot sell your way into being a trusted advisor.

Your sales and marketing messages need to be aligned, because the marketing materials are there when you can't speak for yourself.

SECTION VIII

Start with Your Skills

fourteen

Learning the Ways

A great leader's courage to fulfill his vision
comes from passion, not position.
—John Maxwell

There is no substitute or shortcut for learning to think like any particular Way. If you're that Way Three engineer with a great idea and an entrepreneurial streak, that Way Two vice president ready to become a Way One, or a recent college graduate ready to build the next Facebook, Nike, or five-star restaurant, then you have to start with the skills you already have. There are no shortcuts for experience and the perspective that it brings.

> There are no shortcuts for experience and the perspective that it brings.

If you read *Good to Great* ten years ago, there were doubtless many lessons you took away from it. But if you read it again today, after accumulating ten years of experience, skills, and knowledge, then you will inevitably see lessons in there that you missed the first time. You will see it from a new perspective.

It's like hearing a song from your college days twenty years later. You'll find it doesn't mean the same thing you thought it meant in your twenties. I'm not saying your interpretation is wrong when you're twenty-two. It's just that after twenty more years of living—relationships, ups, downs, deaths, marriage, children—you'll see things from a different perspective. You might appreciate the nuance of the lyrics or realize that what you thought was a "declaration of eternal truth" in the lyrics was actually sung with a sense of irony or sarcasm.

Only when you occupy a Way seat will you know best how to hone the skills that a particular Way must have. But that doesn't mean you have to be a Way One before you can know how to be a Way One. It's not a catch-22. As mentioned before, just because you're a Way Three at work doesn't mean you can't be a Way One in some outside organization or vice versa. And not every great Way Two makes a good Way One, but if you're fortunate enough to be a Way Two who can be mentored by a qualified Way One, it can help develop you as a Way One. But there's no guarantee. Jack Welch of GE mentored four different executives, and his hand-picked replacement, Jeffrey Robert Immelt, while successful, stands forever in Welch's shadow. (Ironically, one of the other three went on to become CEO of Home Depot, which has done well under his leadership.)

There's no one answer. Imagine how very differently Nolan Ryan, as the Way One owner of the Texas Rangers, operates his team from the how the late, iconic George Steinbrenner ran the New York Yankees. Ryan has been a celebrated player and manager. His own manager, Ron Washington, is a former professional player. Steinbrenner, meanwhile, was involved in ownership and investment in teams from almost the time he left the US Air Force until he took ownership of the Yankees, but he never played once as a professional or even minor leaguer.

While there is a Way One of doing things, there is no one Way One of doing things. So there's no shortcut or substitute for experience.

However, there is Return on Energy.

From the beginning I've said that this is a translational tool, a decoder of sorts. You can use it to translate everything in the business world. It's a means of seeing the world that, once employed,

> This is a translational tool, a decoder of sorts. You can use it to translate everything in the business world.

can't be unseen. It's the ability to see the man behind the curtain in every individual, to see the source of strong and weak arrows. It's the tool for increasing ROE because you're going to the core of the challenge or the problem and using a universal language unencumbered by cultural baggage, business jargon, or the smokescreens employed by those who seek to obfuscate rather than illuminate.

In this way, the ROE methodology can be the tool you bring to the table no matter where you are in your career. It's the Intel inside. Shrink-wrapping this book with other business books helps to enhance the reader's understanding of the materials. I recently taught a class at a local university. One of the students said to me that her boss made everyone read *Good to Great*. She went on to say that she didn't understand the book until after learning about Return on Energy. I understood the gravity of that statement and took it as a huge compliment. A poem or a piece of artwork will have multiple meanings beyond the intent of the artist. But in business, if there are multiple interpretations of business methods, how would you ever get everyone on the same page? ROE gets people talking. Sometimes that is enough to move the needle on employee engagement.

When we discussed what a Way One is, the word that kept popping up again and again was "vision." And we discussed how that doesn't mean that the Way One is off lost in the clouds in idea-land. The new "operational" organizational chart we use does resemble a pie, but it resembles more of a classic bull's-eye. And guess who is at the center?

The Way One has to align business objectives to his or her vision. And vision is comprised of core values, core purpose, and the mission of the company. The arrow between the Way One and Way Twos should be embedded with the vision.

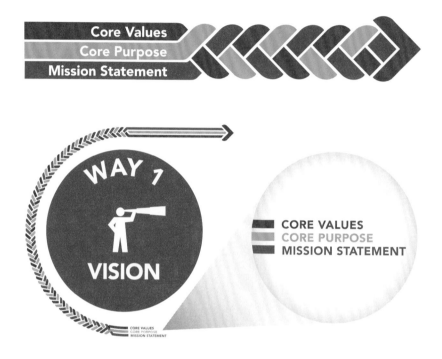

It also helps that the Way One is a conceptual thinker. On Wikipedia this is defined as:

"Problem solving or thinking based on the cognitive process of conceptualization; a process of independent analysis in the creative search for new ideas or solutions, which takes as its starting point that none of the constraints of 'today's reality' need necessarily apply to or shape the future. Thus it does not accept received wisdom, the status quo, or inertia as necessary determinants."

Conceptual thinking can be a valuable analytic or problem-solving tool in any field, but most of all in leadership. It is the ability to understand a situation or problem by identifying patterns or connections and addressing key underlying issues. Conceptual thinking includes the integration of issues and factors into a conceptual framework. It involves using past professional or technical training and experience, creativity, inductive reasoning, and intuitive processes that lead to potential solutions or viable alternatives that may not be obviously relatable or easily identified. Enterprise might consider consulting with entrepreneurs for this reason alone.

Way One thinking requires a mind open to new ways of seeing the world and a willingness to explore. But once the work of analysis is completed and a new concept or mind map emerges, the hard work of communicating this new vision begins. Conceptual thinkers, if they are to succeed, must understand that new, and to many people, unfamiliar, ideas need nurturing and support.

The Way One has already removed the commonly held constraints, but Way Twos and Threes sometimes have problems seeing that the walls of the box have been removed. This is where the Way One is relied upon to provide people development in addition to business results. Part of a Way One's job is to refine in his Way Twos and Way Threes those skills and characteristics of outside-the-box thinking with something so new and unique that it is driven from within.

ROE is that translational tool with which to read leadership materials, whether they are put out by Kubby or the Harvard Business School, so that you can decipher what they mean to you. If I'm a Way Two getting ready to become a Way One I hope I've been mentored or have invested in myself enough to learn ways of leadership. I may start with an ROE Gap, but I will close that gap quickly because I've done it before, for myself and those that I have managed. Leaders will align the vision with strategy, and leaders should understand if you take care of the little things, the big things will take care of themselves.

Way Ones understand that, aside from leadership, the budding Way One has to understand organizational behavior and then step outside of their slice of pie and step into the nucleus, and while they are the marketing SME, they are also responsible for sales, finance, legal, operations, and any other areas of the company that will impact the business results.

Now that they are leading the people managing the Way Threes, they can't be SMEs. You see, Jason Garrett, the head coach of the Dallas Cowboys, is also calling the plays. He's the offensive coordinator, a Way Two role—he's the Way One also filling in a Way Two role. He can't be in all offensive coordinator meetings and be the head coach of team very easily. If he's a great offensive coordinator but not giving the team leadership, he's not doing his job as a Way One. If he's a better offensive coach than head coach, what is he doing to develop himself as a head coach? Who mentored him? Are they a qualified Way One? What was done to develop him for this role? Why should results determine qualification?

Are people leaders by nature or do we train and teach leadership? I'm sure it's both. Some people have that natural leadership ability and some don't. If I have a mediocre Way Two with natural leadership and an outstanding Way Two without it, then something needs to change. Leadership needs to be nurtured, and a Way One has to invest a lot in mentoring. The question the Way One must ask herself is, "Is it worth the ROE?"

In established companies, as we saw with GE, it may be that the process of mentoring a new Way One needs to happen sooner rather than later. An overlap of vision between the first generation and the second needs to be extended as much as possible to avoid falling into the mind-set of "the first generation builds it, the second generation enjoys it, the third generation destroys it." That's not to say a company should be static in its vision, but

> What influences who we are five years from now? It's the people we meet and the understanding of the books we read.

a continuity of vision in the leadership is important to long-term health.

What influences our vision? What influences who we are five years from now? It's the people we meet and the understanding of the books we read. These are two things we can take charge of right here, right now, regardless of whether you're a career Way Two, a tech school dropout with a billion-dollar idea, or someone who just wants to fulfill their dream of starting their own small business—that beachfront grill or that auto repair shop.

The ROE methodology gives you the tools to analyze yourself and your own team and see what Way they are thinking.

If you use the ROE methodology to translate everything that's out there, you will see and better understand things that you never noticed before.

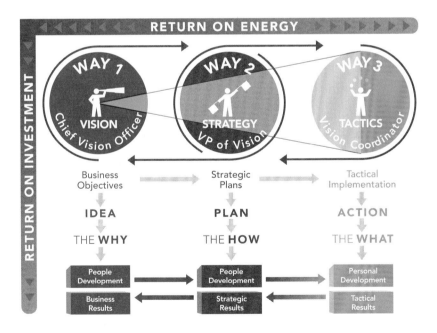

epilogue

The ROE Movement

What if everyone was thinking and communicating the ROE Way? What if everyone was sitting in the right seats? What if, also, their positions were properly aligned to their job titles and they were communicating with people aligned in the ROE Way? What would the results be of that department or company? What if two companies, say a customer and vendor, both employed an ROE culture? I am obviously very passionate about ROE, so what if two countries employed ROE?

To say we are competing in difficult economic times is the understatement of the year. With ROE:

- We can improve our schools one student at a time, one teacher at a time, one principal at a time, *one school district at a time.*
- We can improve the quality of our society one family member at a time, one household at a time, one city at time, one state at a time, *one country at a time.*
- We can improve this economy one employee at a time, one division at a time, *one company at a time.*

- We can improve world relations one constituent at a time, one congressman, senator, and governor at time, and *one president at a time.*

Get my point? You see, if you take care of the little things, the big things take care of themselves. There has never been a simple process to take an idea to action. In fact, as we have pointed out, the twentieth-century thinking is, "An idea without action is a pipe dream." Now we know there is a better Way. ROE states, "An idea without a plan is a pipe dream." I am proud to have said that, certainly not for my benefit, but for yours. I love speaking to motivated people who can hear the ROE benefits and take it and make it their own. I love the emails I get after a speaking engagement from people who learned the ROE methodology and how it benefited them. They have sat in many of the above seats in the "We can improve" statements. I dream of a US president running on a "We can improve platform" and having the campaign *powered by ROE.* What is their vision for our country? What strategies have they outlined to achieve the results to accomplish the vision? What tactically is being done on a daily basis that we can ultimately tie back to that original promise, their vision? I would ask: Do you buy in to the vision, only to get confused with the strategies and get buried in a million details, which usually confuse and not support the vision that won your vote?

Whether you support President Obama or not, he said in his last State of the Union address, "The first step to winning the future is encouraging American innovation." In fact, he used the word "innovation" or "innovate" eleven times. I disagree with President Obama. The ROE followers know that the *first* step is vision. Vision supports innovation. ROE breathes life into innovation. Innovation is the second step. Let's get this basic terminology straight: the ROE methodology is proven to implement the vision. Starbucks did not start with innovation;

they started with the vision to create "the place" between your home and work. Innovation came second.

I am a big proponent of the American business. I have owned my own business for over fifteen years and spent all of my childhood and young adult life through high school working in my parents' business. I have belonged to the Entrepreneur Organization (www.eonetwork.org) for the past six years and have personally benefited greatly from being an active member. We hear all the time that small business will get people working again, get the country back on track. Enterprises are conserving cash and not hiring; small businesses cannot get cash to hire. What is wrong with this picture?

It's this: it's popular to say, "I believe in and support small businesses," but how much confidence is there in the people actually running these businesses when the failure rate is so high? I am concerned by what they are teaching the new entrepreneurial students today. I am very passionate to educate people on the ROE Way. To support my ROE vision we are strategizing on an ROE textbook for entrepreneurial education. Business ethics has taken a *huge* hit over the last decade or so. Why then do 80 percent or more of small business fail? Why do only 15 percent of small businesses generate wealth and the rest generate a meager lifestyle for the owners and employees? No one has come up with a better Way. For all of our technological advances, *only* people can come up with an idea. People in businesses need serious help capitalizing on ideation. ROE can help.

> It's popular to say, "I believe in and support small businesses," but how much confidence is there in the people actually running these businesses when the failure rate is so high?

In the book *The Presentation Secrets of Steve Jobs* is a line that states, "Never underestimate the power of a vision so simple that it can fit on a napkin." Or maybe put in the twenty-first century, "Never underestimate the power of a vision that can be typed in 140 characters or less." We have only scratched the surface of innovation in this country, in the world. The United States is only five hundred years old or so. Look at the innovation curve, which really only kicked in within the past fifty years. Only 10 percent of our country's existence has been on a steep innovation growth trajectory. What is next? Our country is not as old as the Middle East, Africa, and China—not old enough to experience their kinds of problems. I'm amazed when I travel abroad by the dates on documents, buildings, churches, and other landmarks. Our country is a baby compared to these more mature countries. Maturity does not necessarily mean superiority, but with maturity comes responsibility. And we need to be more responsible with the gift in a society that allows us to innovate and profit from it. What will the relationship be between the United States, Mexico, and Canada in a thousand years? What will the relationship be between Pennsylvania and New York in five hundred years, for that matter? Innovation is great, but how far, how fast, *how*?

ROE is a simple process to take idea to action regardless of the stage the business is in on the lifecycle. It's idea, plan, action or vision, strategy, tactics. All ideas have a force behind them, energy that has to be expelled by a lot of people to make it successful to get to the 15 percent "wealth" category. Do you have strong arrows? Are you wearing many hats or jumping from one seat to the next? Do you modify your thinking and communication style as a result or do you expect people to adapt to you? Are your people doing the same thing? Are we connecting the right people to their desired results? Ideas do not have to be game changers; even small ideas that improve an existing process can have dramatic ROI effect.

> ROE is the DNA in ROI and without ROE, ROI will end up DOA

ROE is the DNA in ROI and without ROE, ROI will end up DOA.

Why do over 80 percent of businesses fail in the first five years? Why do only 15 percent of businesses generate wealth? Like we have said, a business is like all living things. Its growth is very predictable, as stated by Ichak Adizes, PhD in the introduction to *Corporate Lifecycles*. Apple is a superior business in its space, in maturity; Harley Davidson might be at death. I have experience in dealing with both. There are a lot of business ideas being born every day and a lot of business ideas dying every day. What is the idea census right now in your business? These ideas need food, love, and attention, just like living things. There is no simple or easy methodology to being a parent. ROE is the simple process to support innovation. Remember, simple does not mean easy.

I believe that ideation will be one of the major forces to help guide us through. I have been interested in inventions for a long time. I loved the show *American Inventor*. *Shark Tank* is now a family favorite. In fact, several years ago, I studied for the patent bar exam. I even took a patent bar study course in Washington DC and toured the United States Patent and Trademark Office because I was so interested in the field. I thought that by passing the patent bar I could help people better market their inventions. It fascinated me to see some of the ideas that have been patent protected and are just sitting on the shelf. I know this is sometimes part of an intellectual property portfolio strategy, but many are from great visionaries or great tacticians who don't know what to do next.

My vision for ROE is to establish an ROE culture in our society. I am honored to speak on my topic. I have the passion to support this movement; do you? Can you see my vision? Will you join me?

My strategy is to execute exciting ROE workshops and consulting programs that integrate learning at all three levels: visual, auditory, and kinesthetic (for people who need to touch and feel). Tactically we have resources in the form of workplace posters, light switch covers ("turn on" ROE), assessment tools, and of course, the book for suggested reading. Plus we have other kinds of ROE tools to support the movement. Various strategic partnerships have been and will continue to be powered by ROE to support the movement. I understand that Way Ones and Twos are the "target market" for the business book market. But I know from real-world personal experience that all the Ways can benefit from learning and embracing ROE. Do you want to accomplish your vision faster? Establish an ROE culture by designating a chief energy officer, the ROE apostle. This is the position I hold in my companies. I realized early that I could not afford *not* to be part of this. My vision under the ROE Movement is to have many chief energy officers who all benefit from each other. Learn more at www.ROEMovement.com.

When visions are aligned and everyone is on the same page, ROE is high and ROI will follow. But what happens if employees' personal visions are not aligned to their employers' visions, at least in the fundamental tenants? What happens if partners' visions are not aligned? What is the personal vision of each of your employees, your direct reports? In other words, is there an ROE alignment? Whether there is a vision or not, I think people settle into a routine of tasks aligned to something. What is your something? Are you going to be ready when the unemployment rate drops and there is an influx of people and ideas in the workplace? How (how = strategy) will *you* benefit? What (what = tactics) are *you* doing to prepare? You have made a great start by reading and implementing ROE in your life. Now go and increase your and someone else's Return on Energy!

about the author

Michael Rose is the founder of Return on Energy Inc. and CEO of both Rose Group Companies–Mojo Media Labs, a strategic marketing agency, and Marketing Candy™, a promotional agency. He also serves as an adjunct professor at Texas Christian University's Extended Education Department and has been a guest speaker at Southern Methodist University.

A scientist by training, teacher by nature, and entrepreneur by spirit and drive, Michael brings both clients and audiences his unique perspective on business organization and communication.

Michael's innovative, game-changing approach, centered around the proprietary concept of Return on Energy™, is born of his unorthodox viewpoint that turns business organizations on their side and teaches leaders and management a new way to achieve personal growth and business success.

Michael brings together generational business lessons and his own empirical, science-based approach in order to build highly engaging work environments. Michael's powerful methodology serves as the focus of this book, which will change how people view their own places in business and life.